Moped Mania
By Thomas Auer

Dedicated to my loving wife and family.

Published in the United States of America

Mopeds are the primary form of transportation in Cambodia and Vietnam. As such, they are used in many unusual ways. This photo journal displays many of these uses seen during a trip to these countries in 2019.

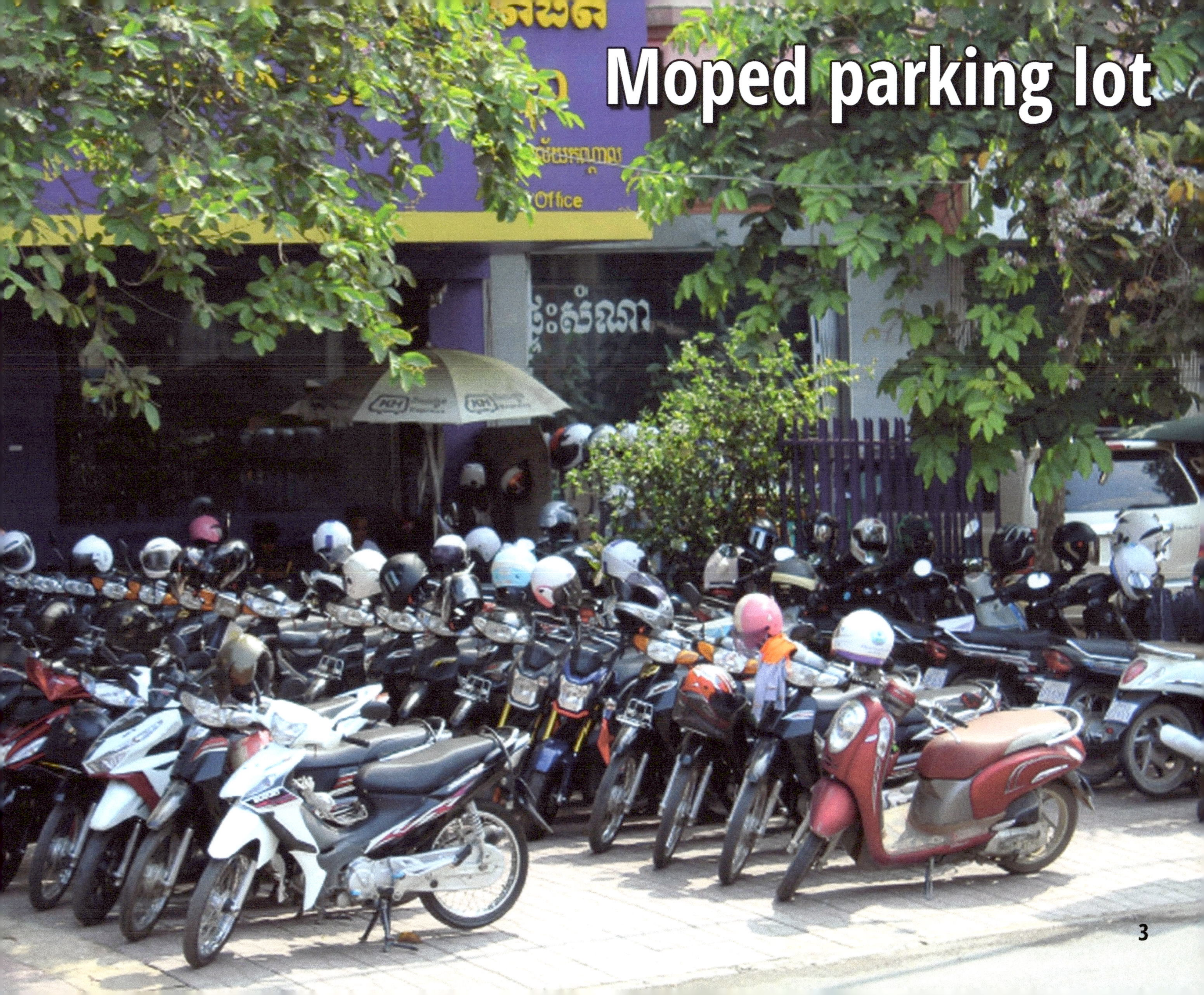

Moped parking lot

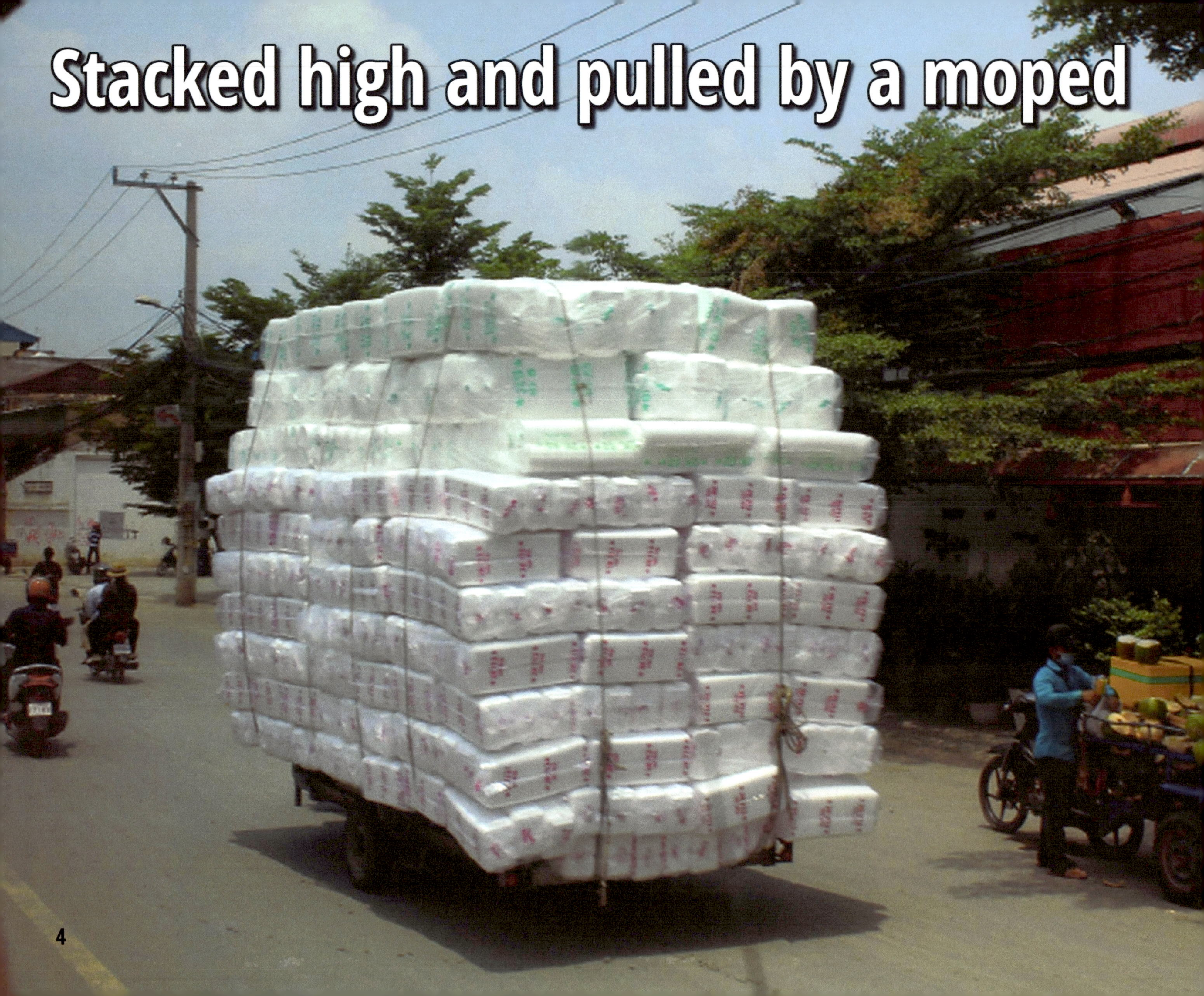

4

Family shopping trip

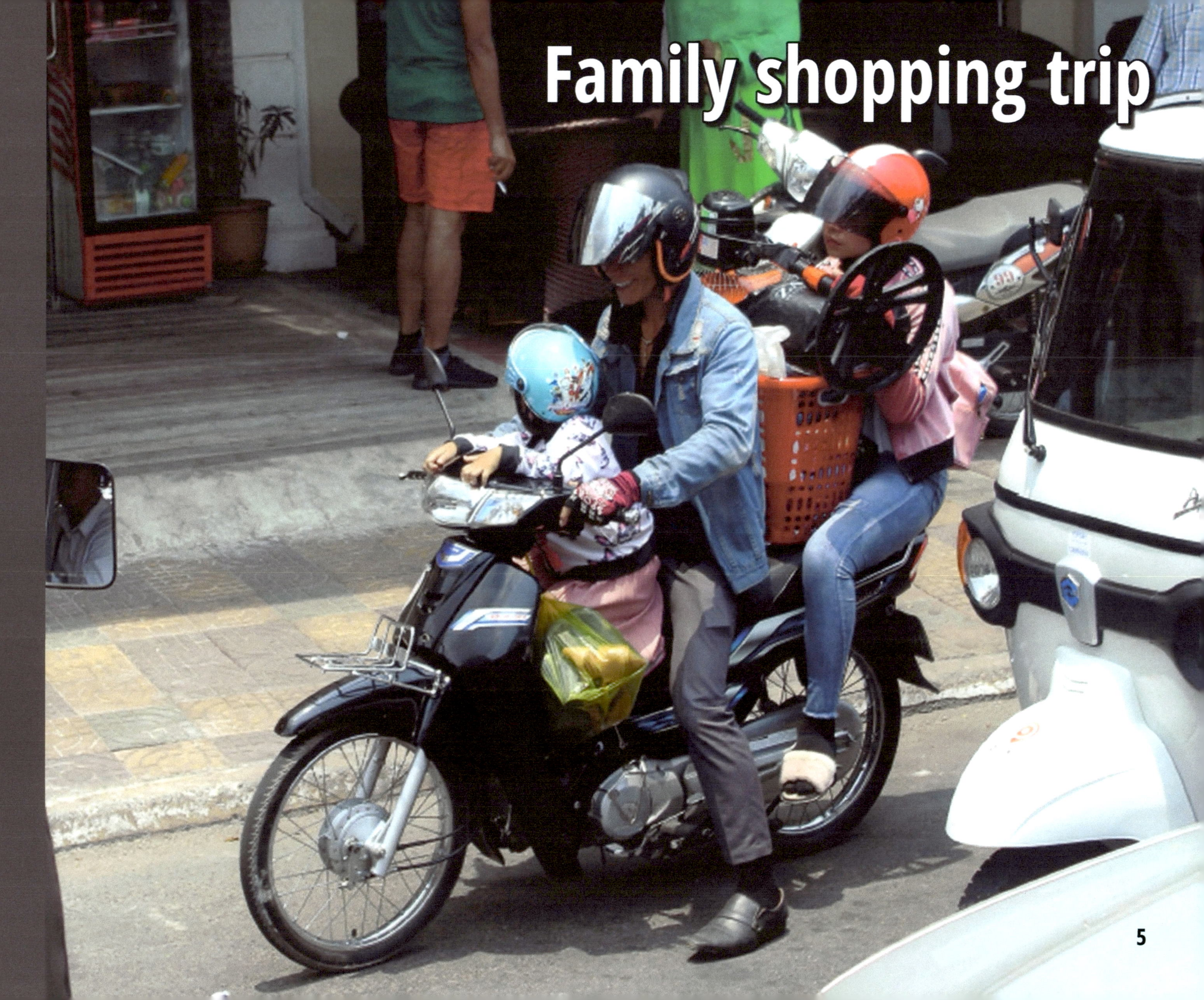

Happy travels

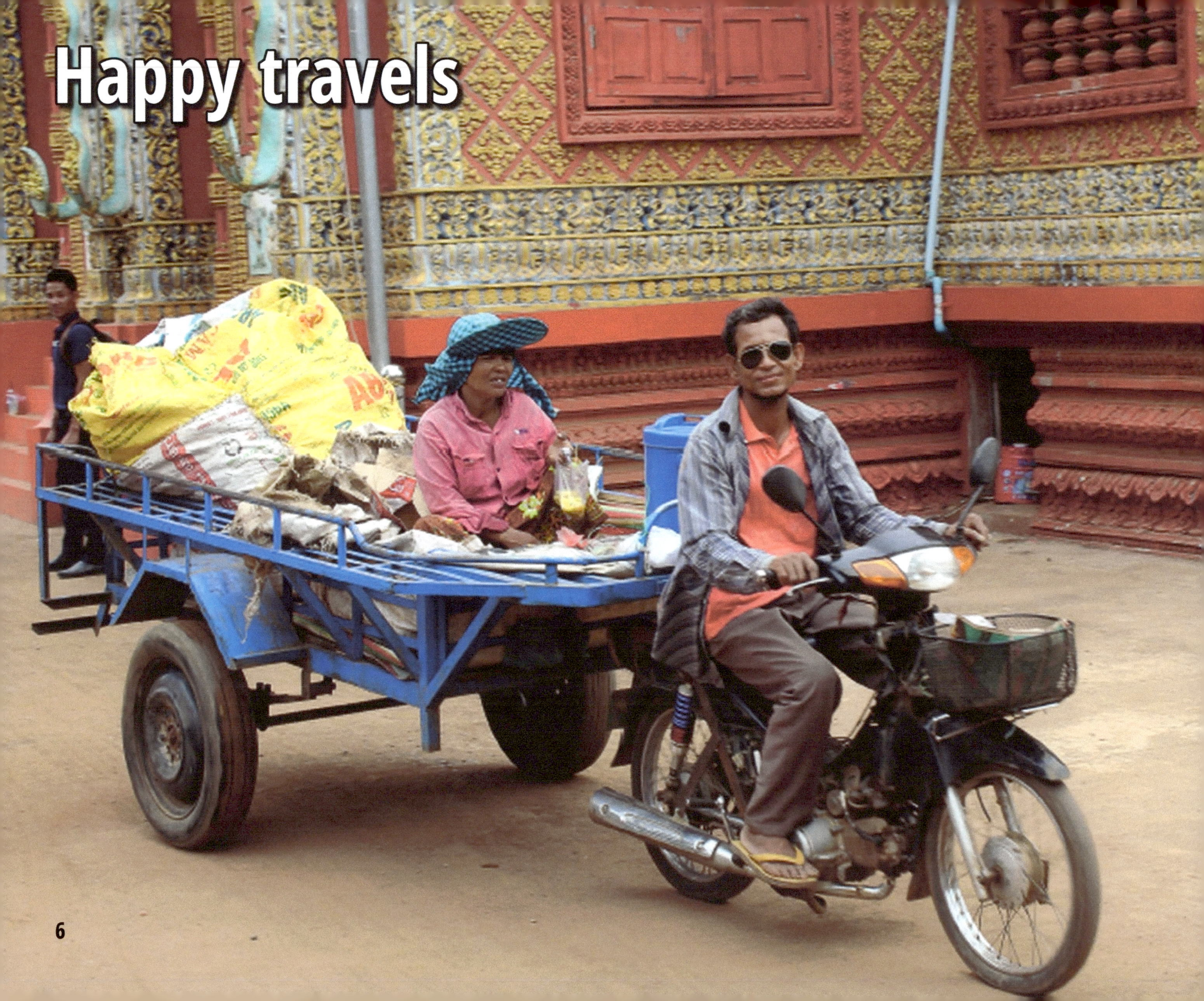

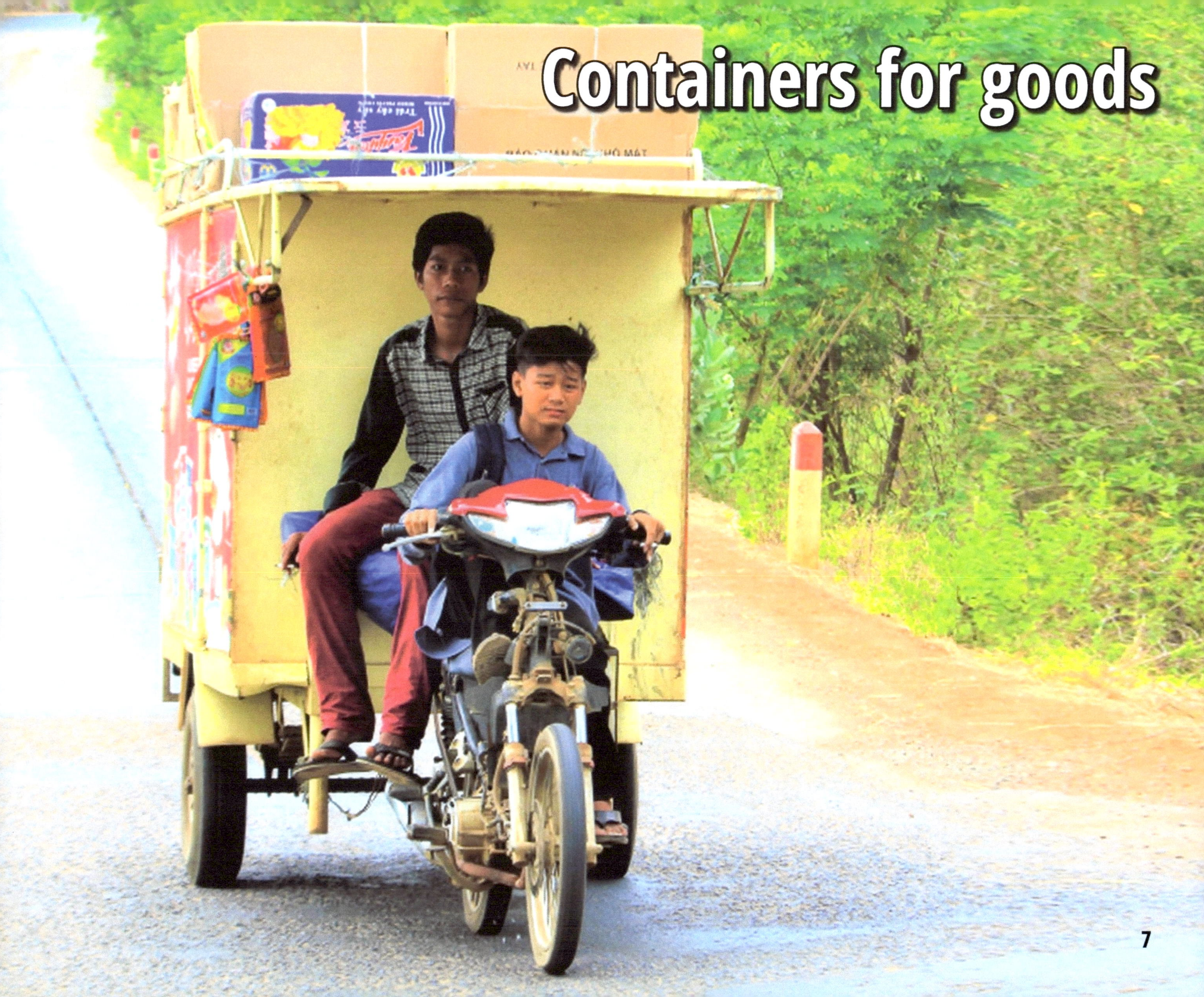
Containers for goods

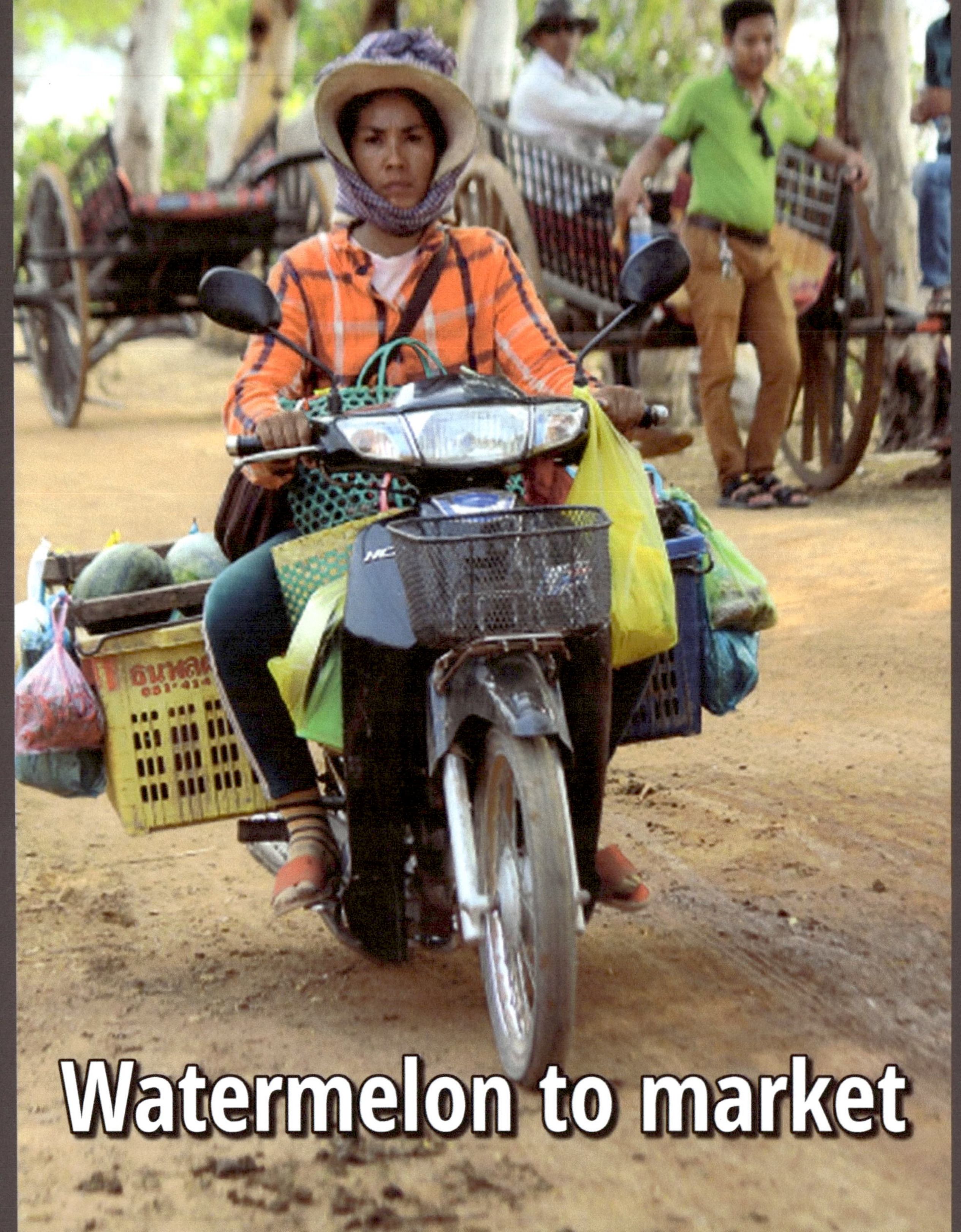

Watermelon to market

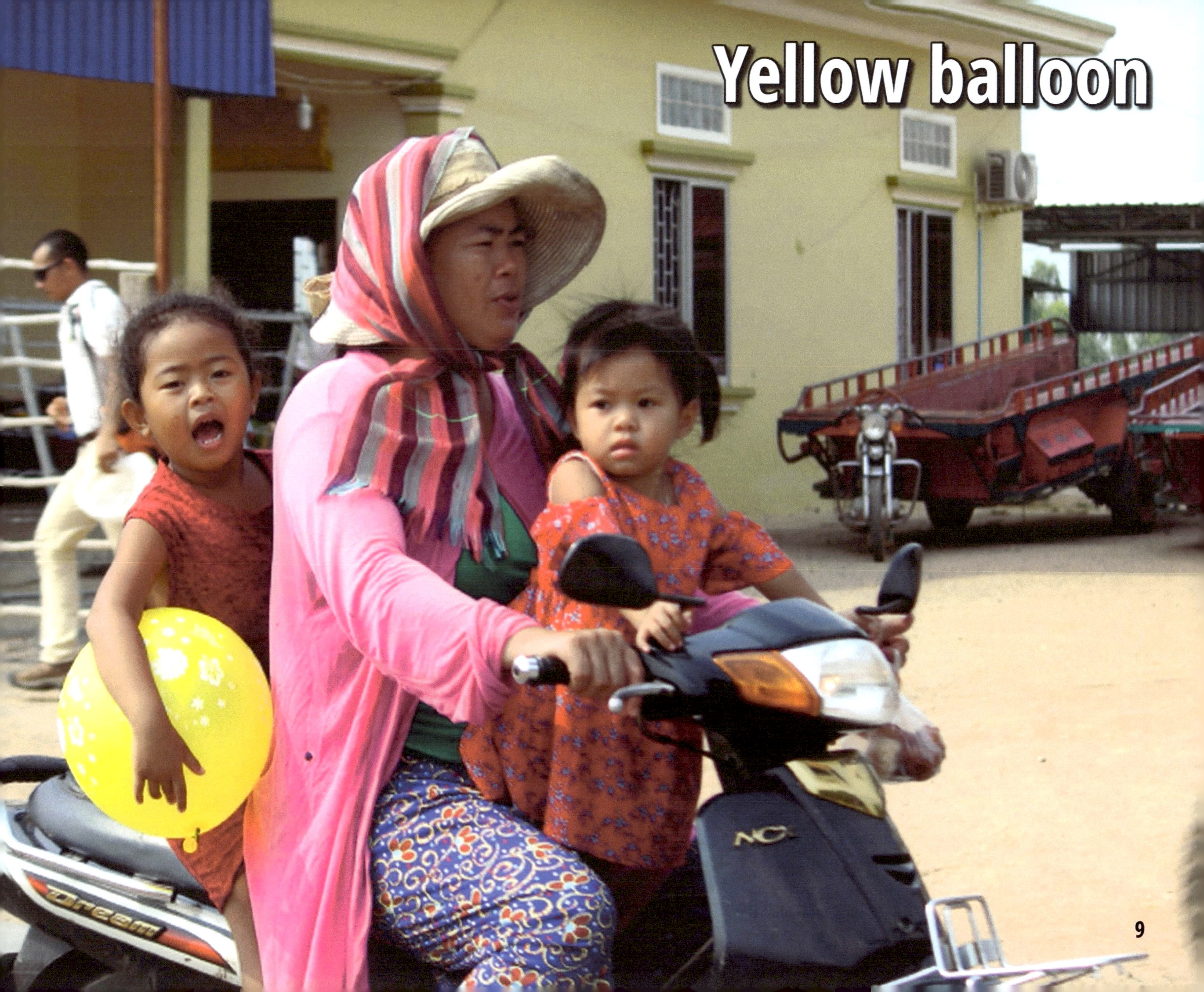
Yellow balloon

Family trip to the town

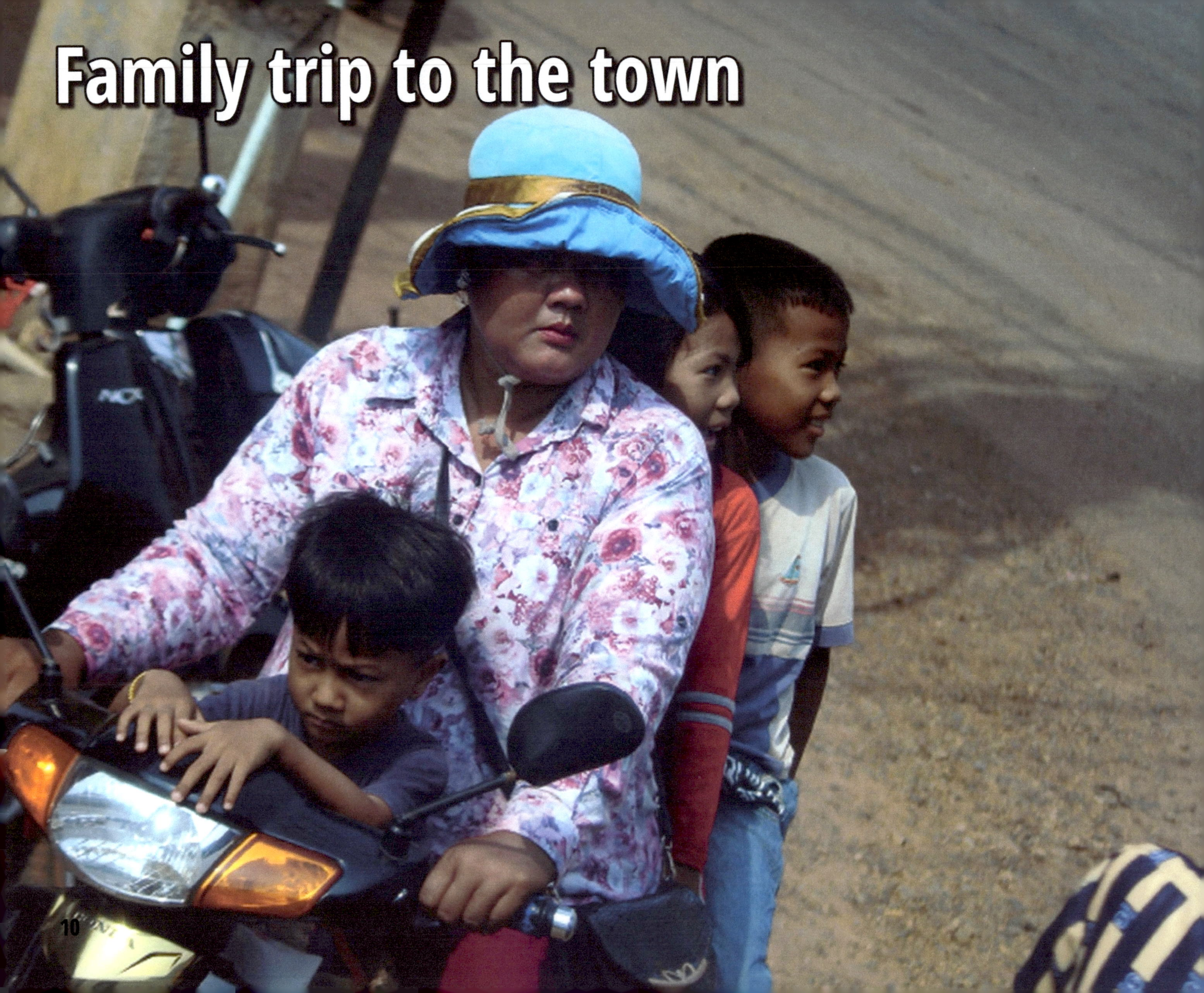

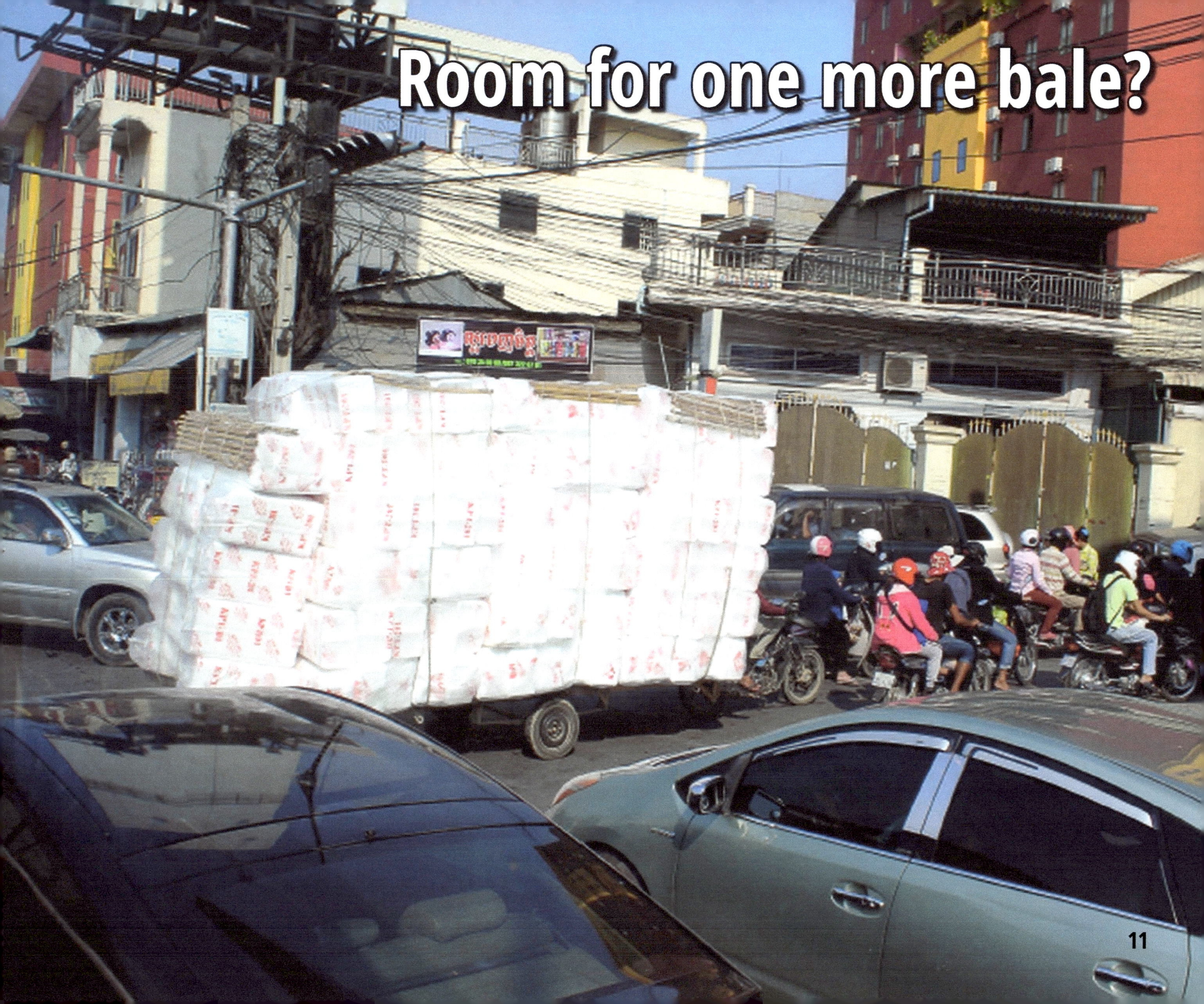
Room for one more bale?

Typical rural gas station

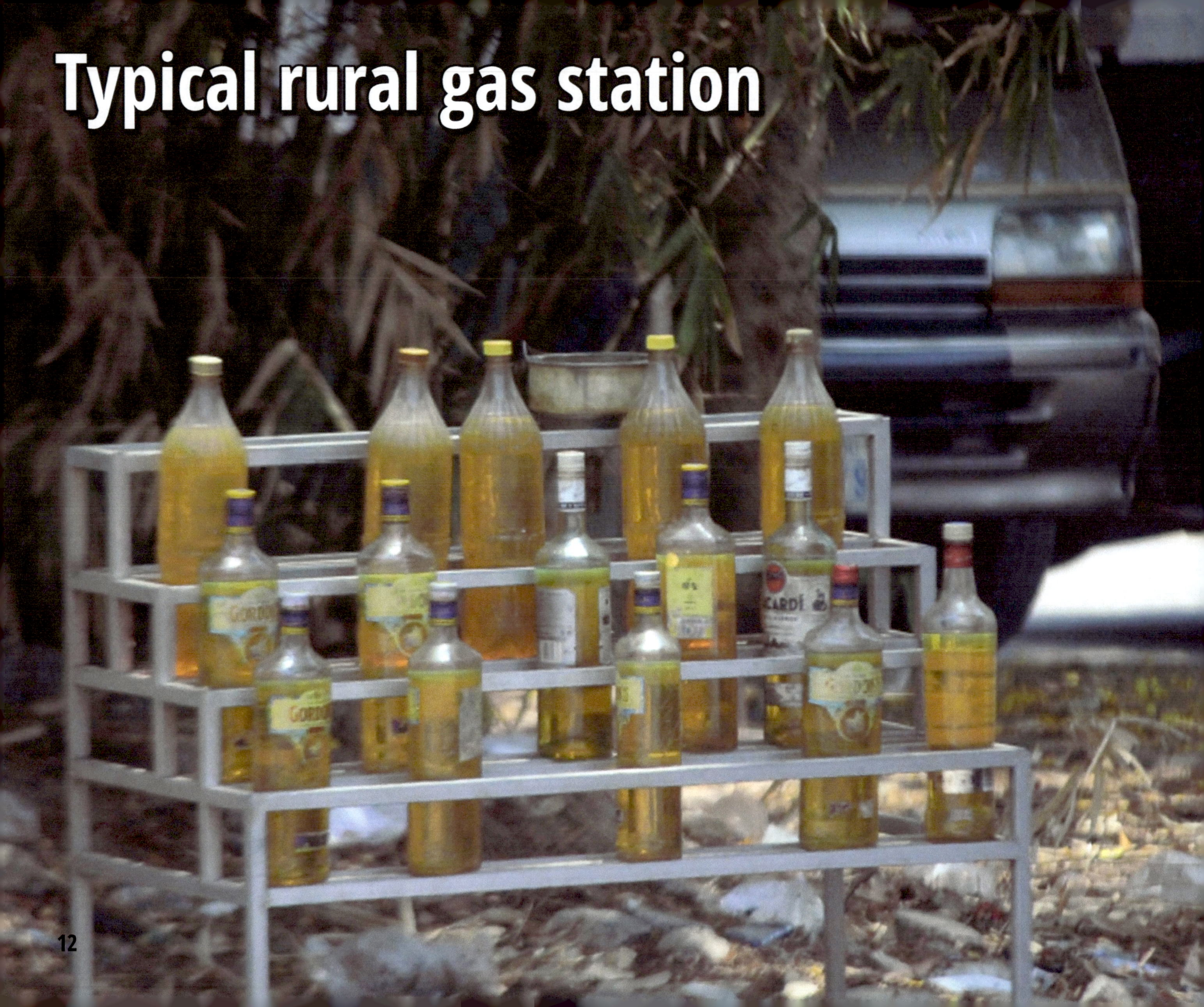

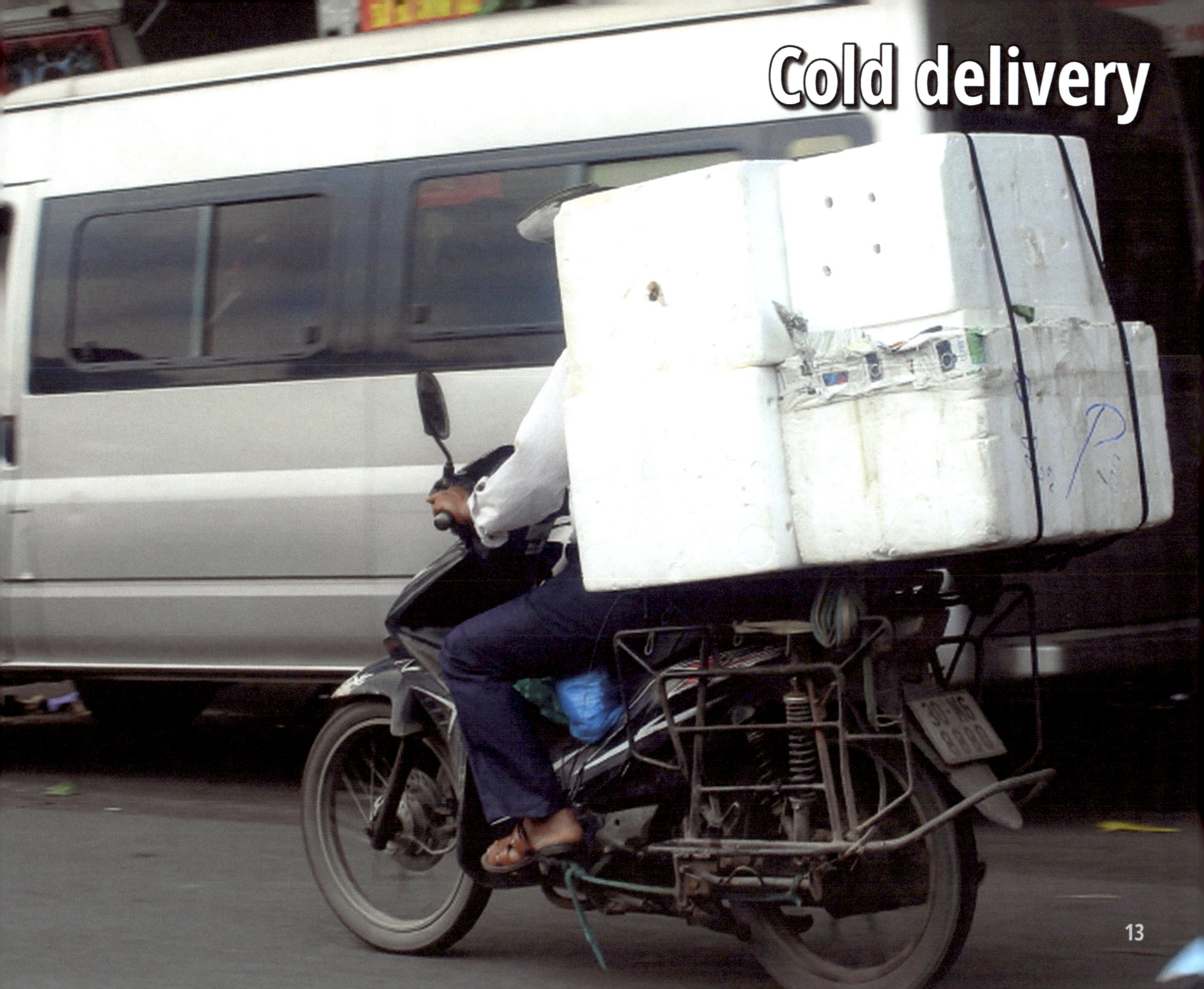

13

Busy downtown street

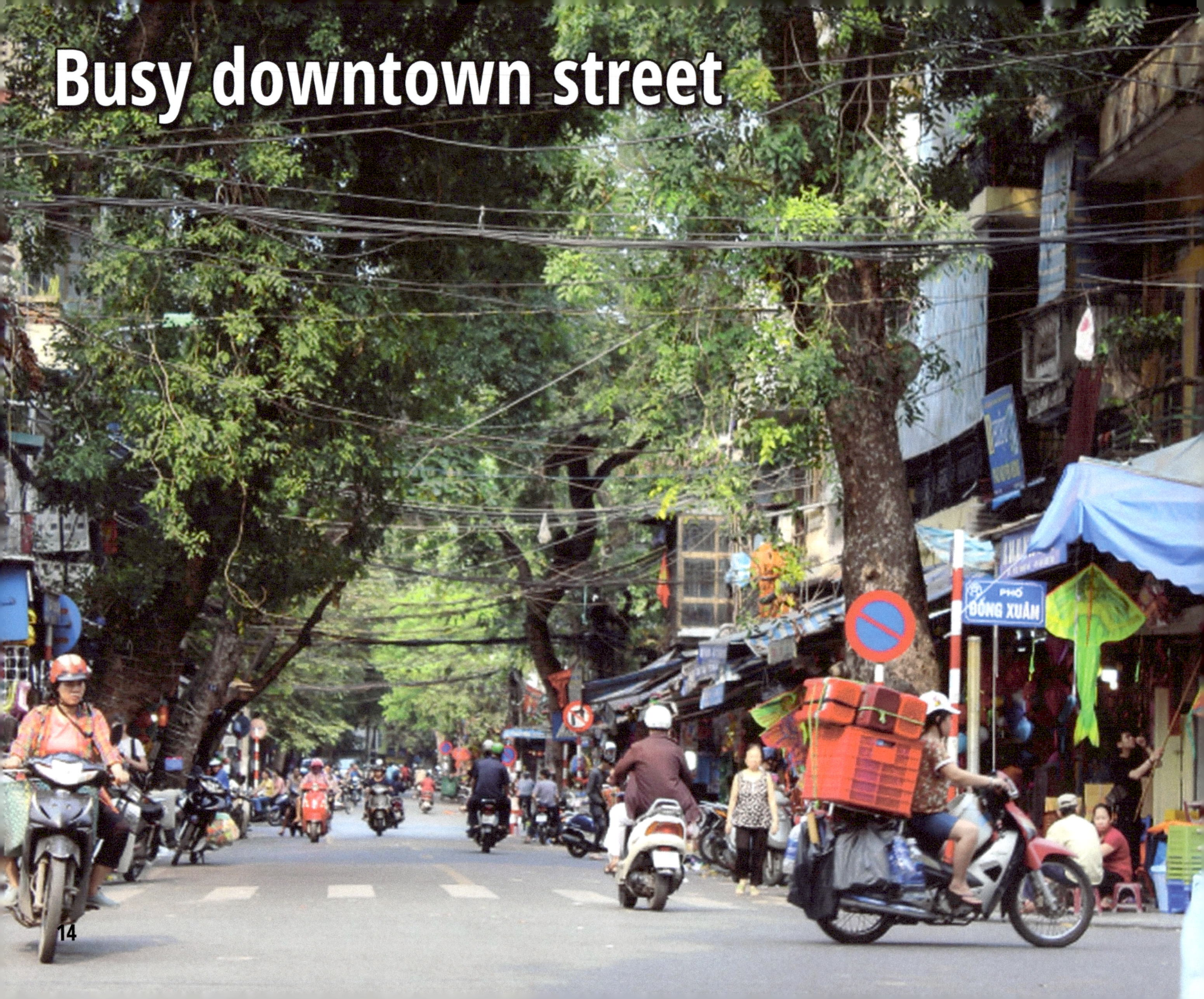

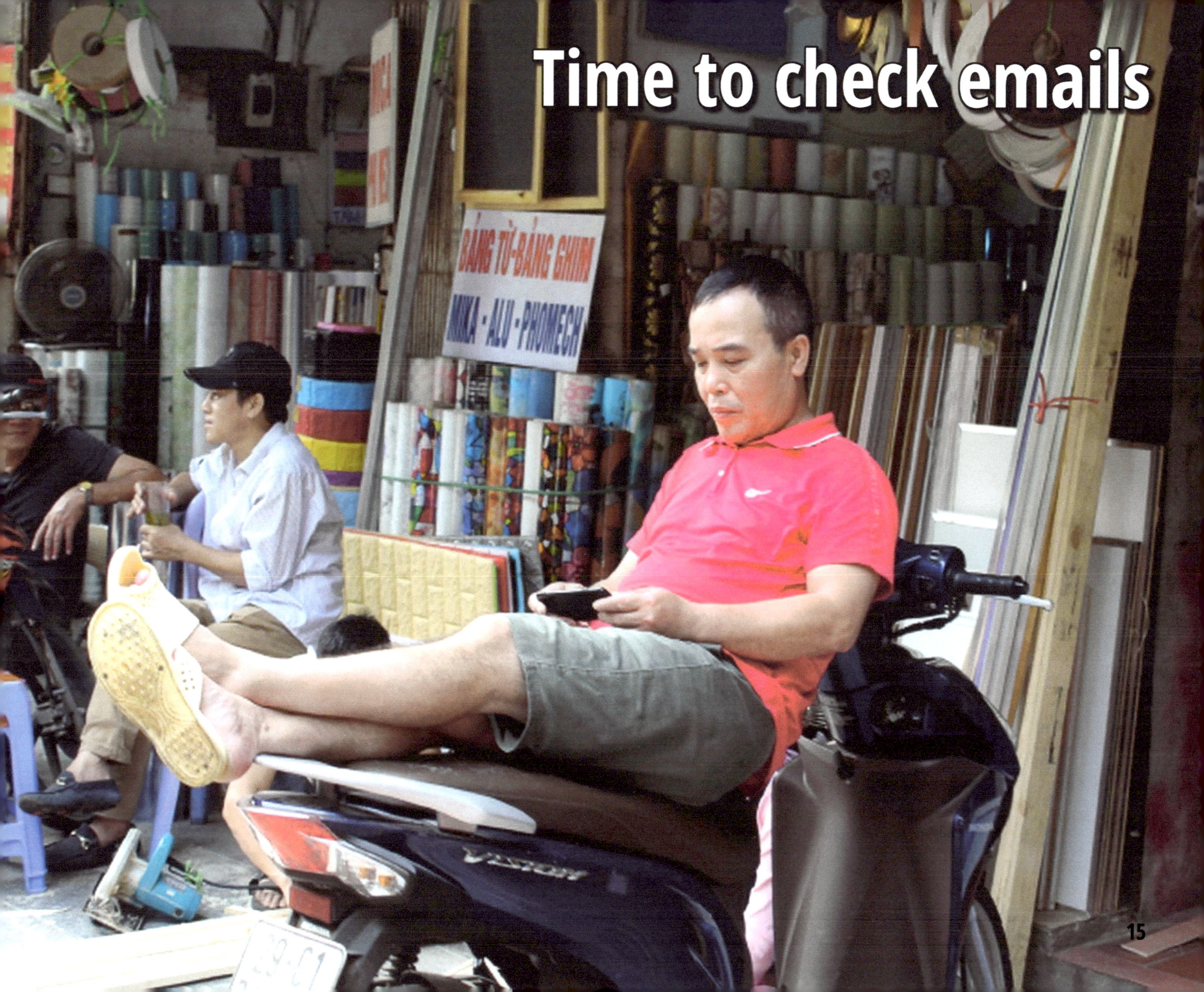
Time to check emails
BẢNG TỪ-BẢNG GHIM
MICA · ALU · PHOMECH

Eggs – really??

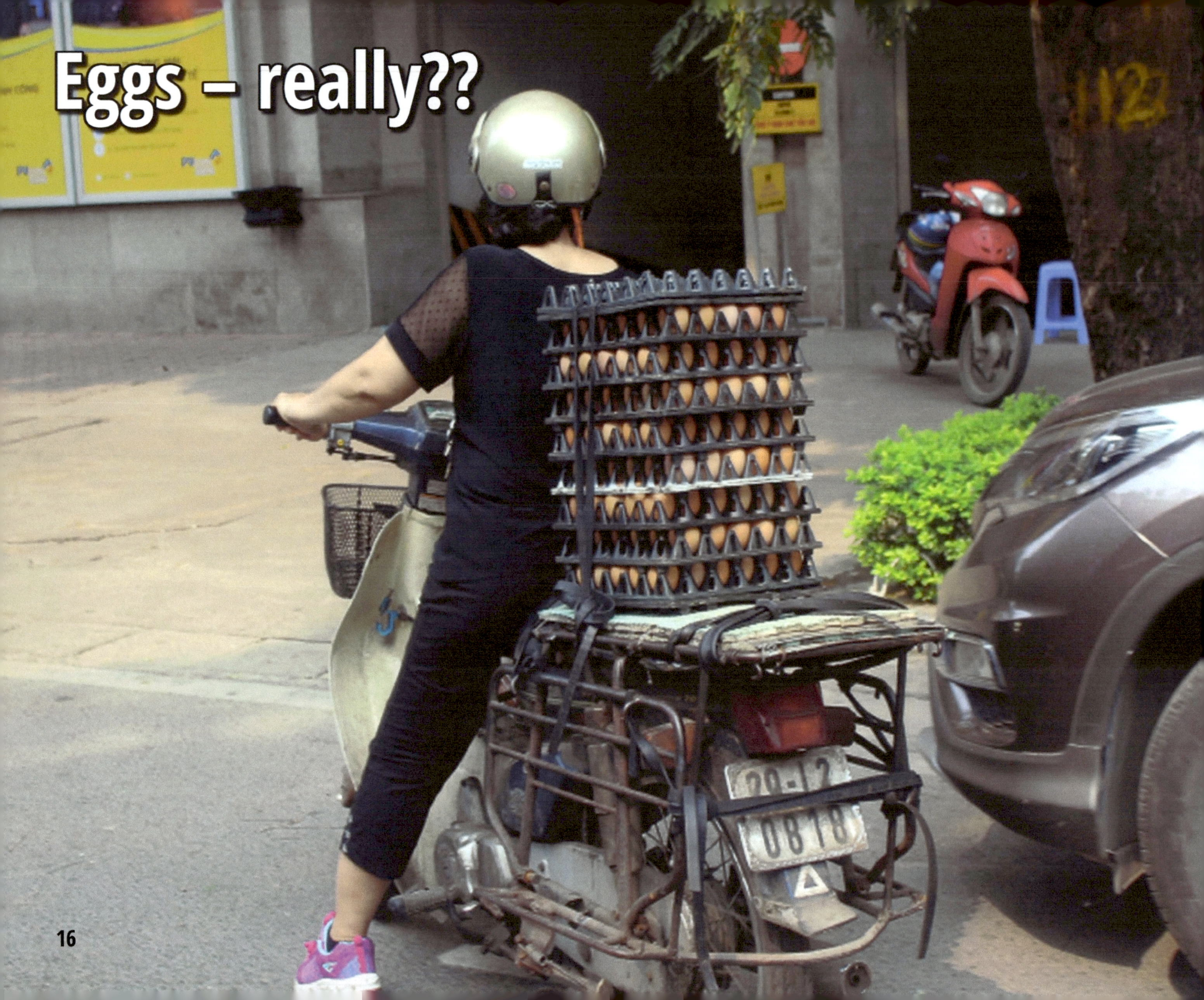

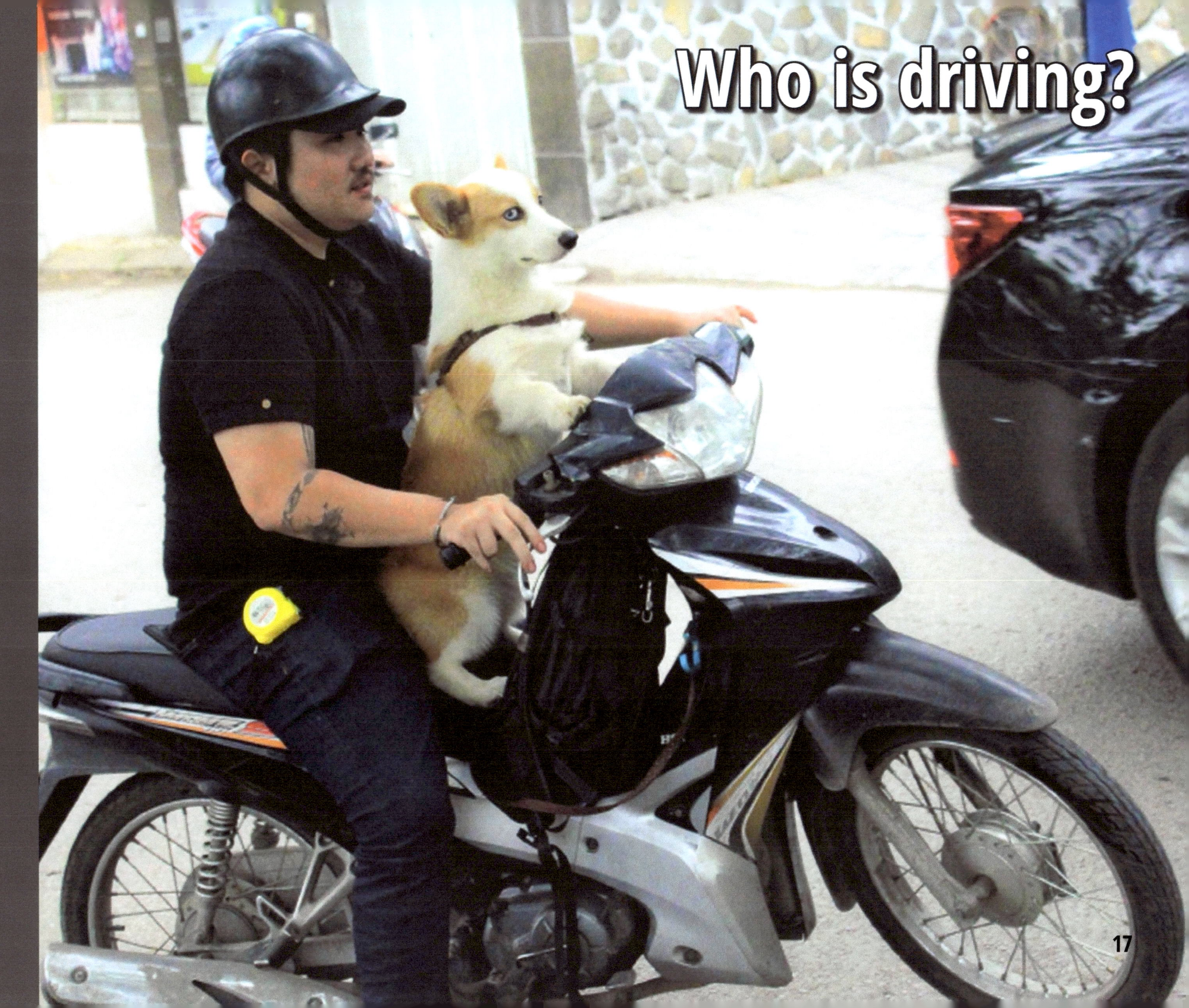
Who is driving?

Covered from the rain?

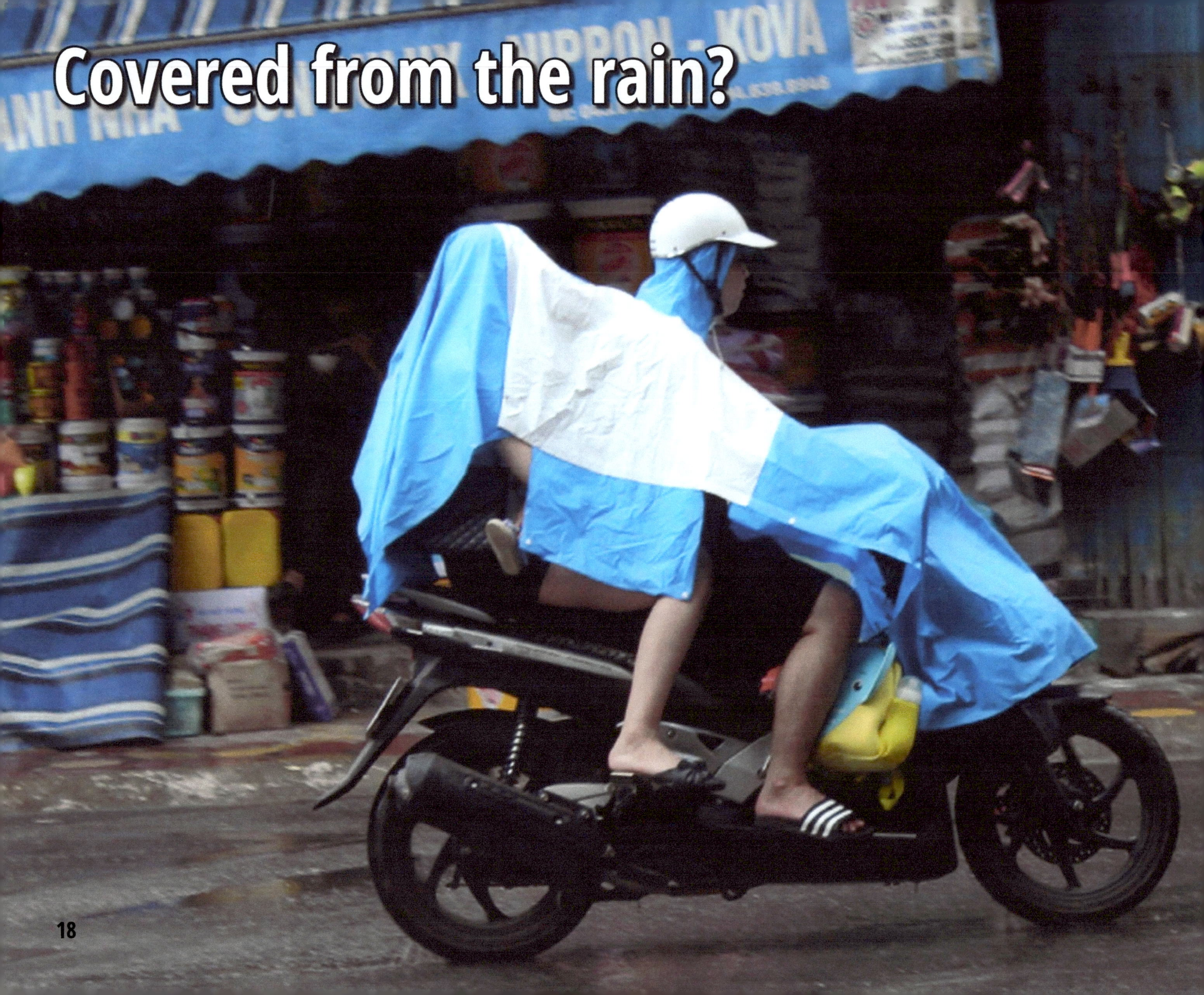

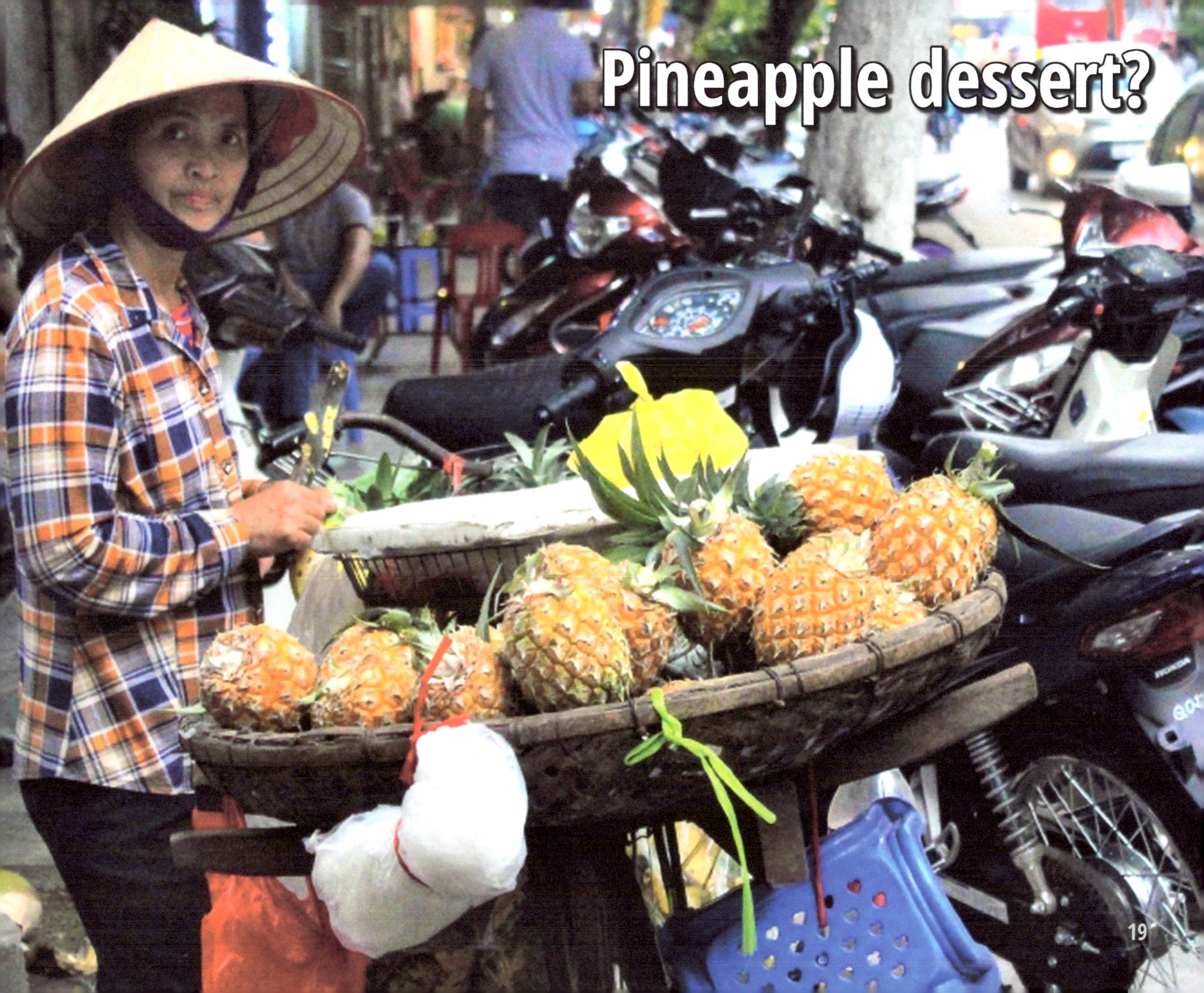
Pineapple dessert?
19

Carrying cases

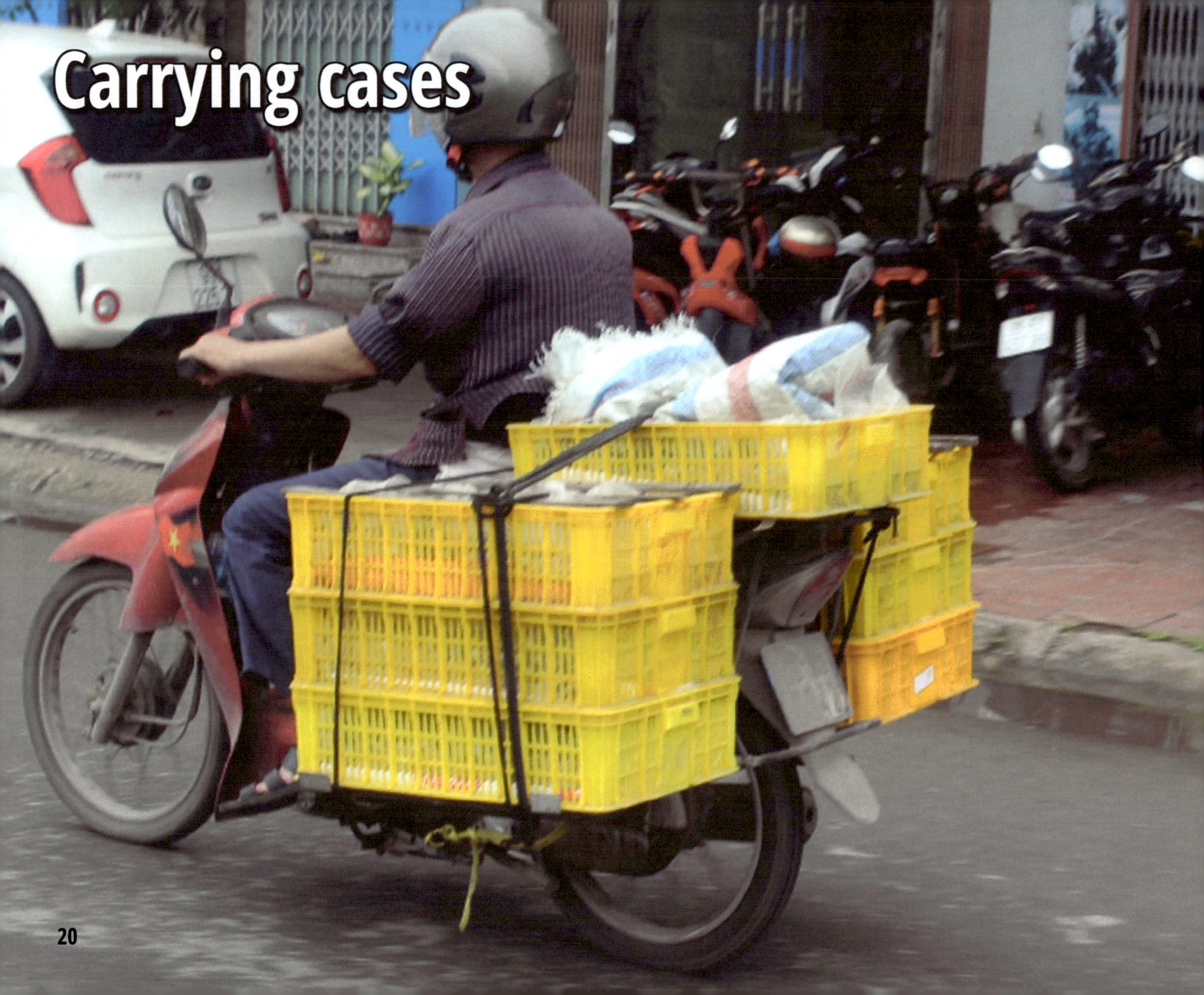

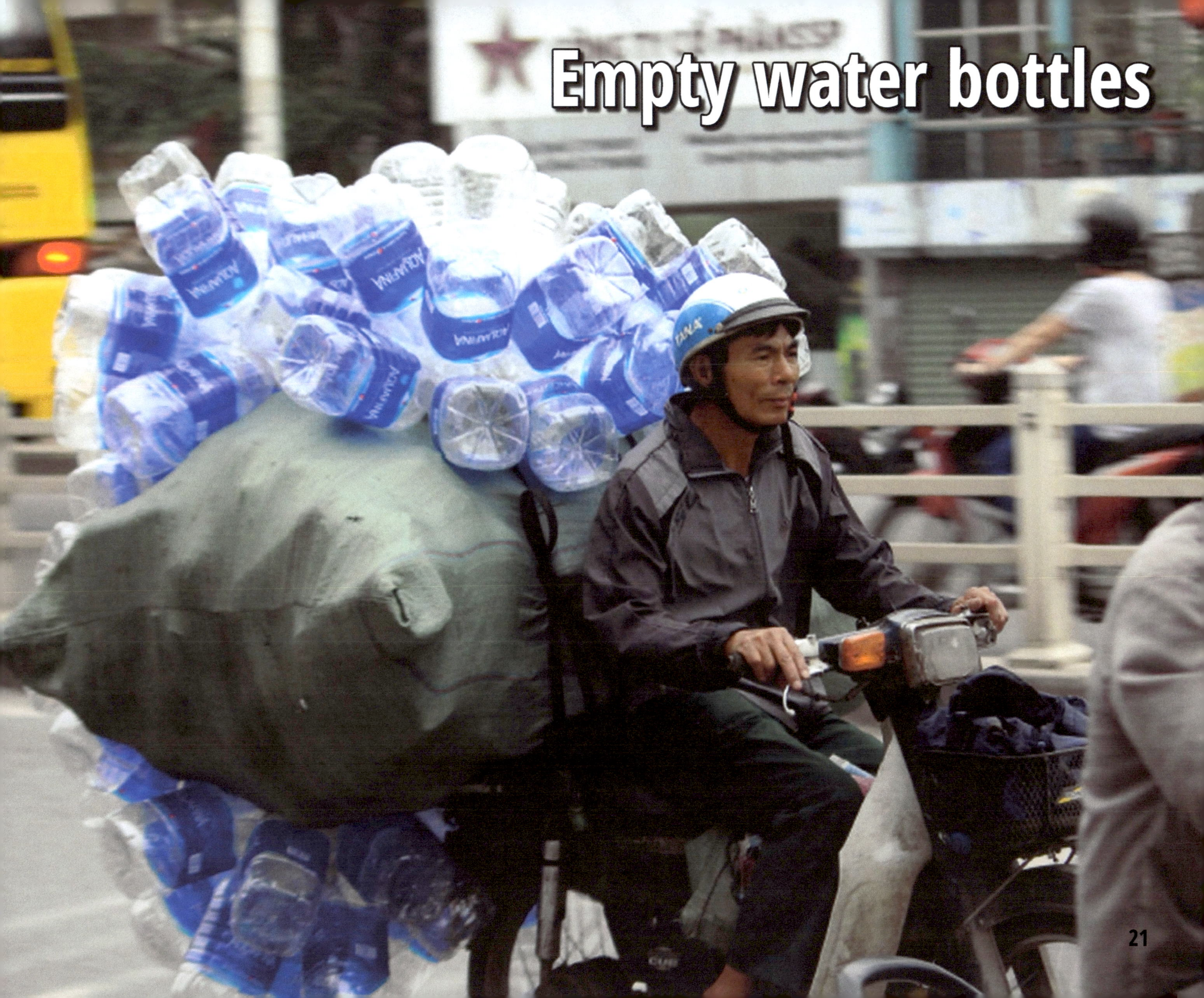

Empty water bottles

Trash pick up

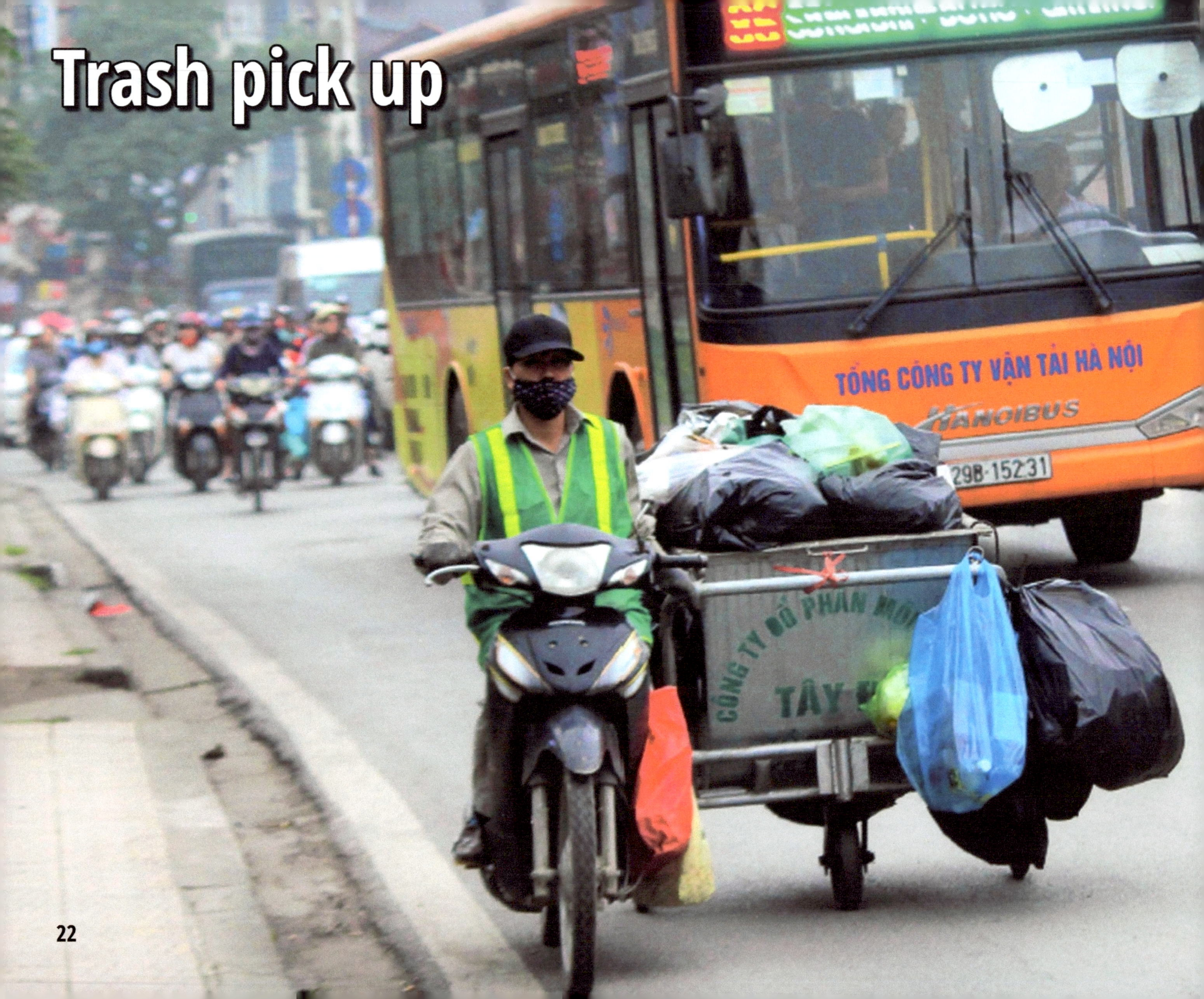

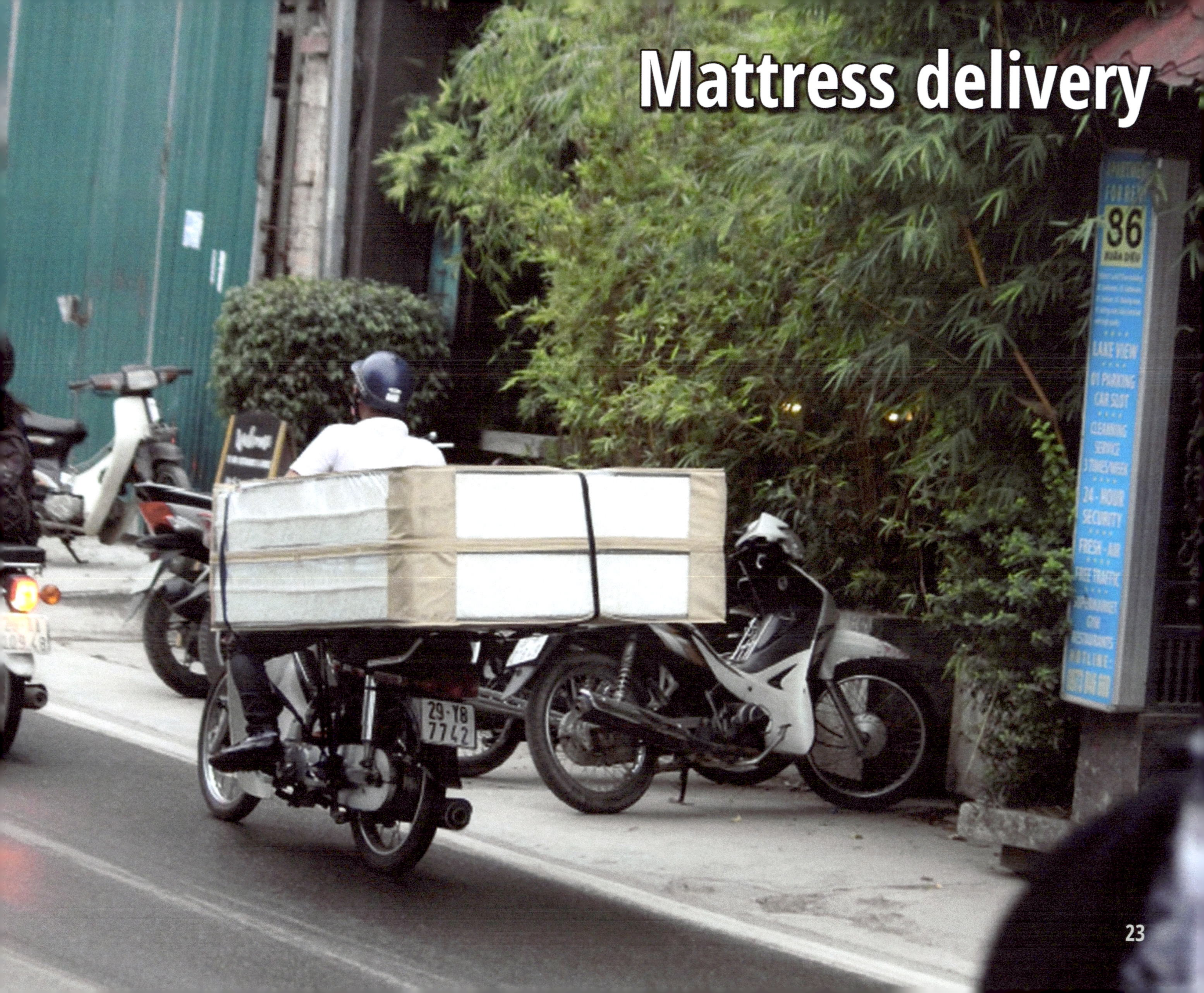

Mattress delivery

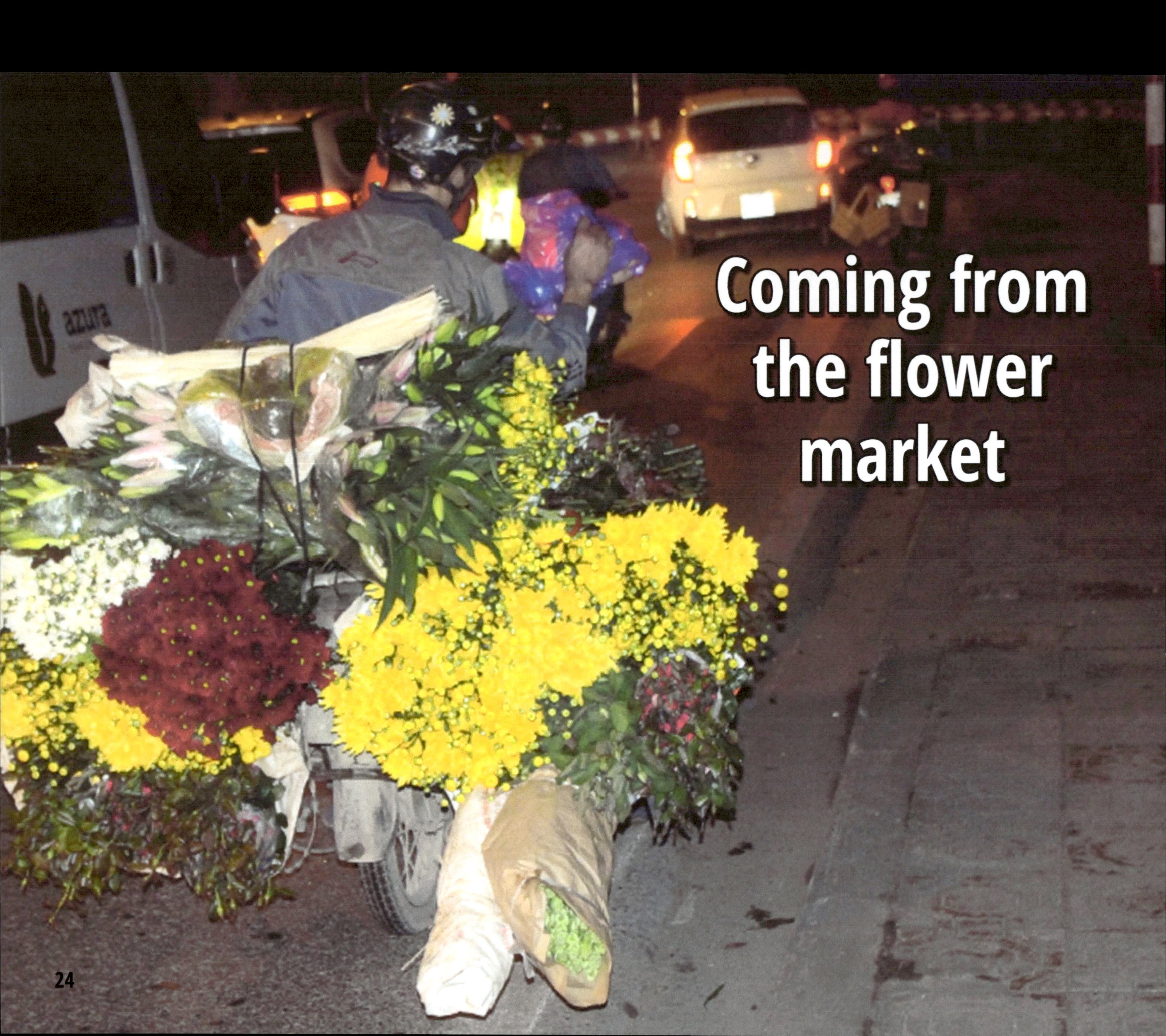

Coming from
the flower
market

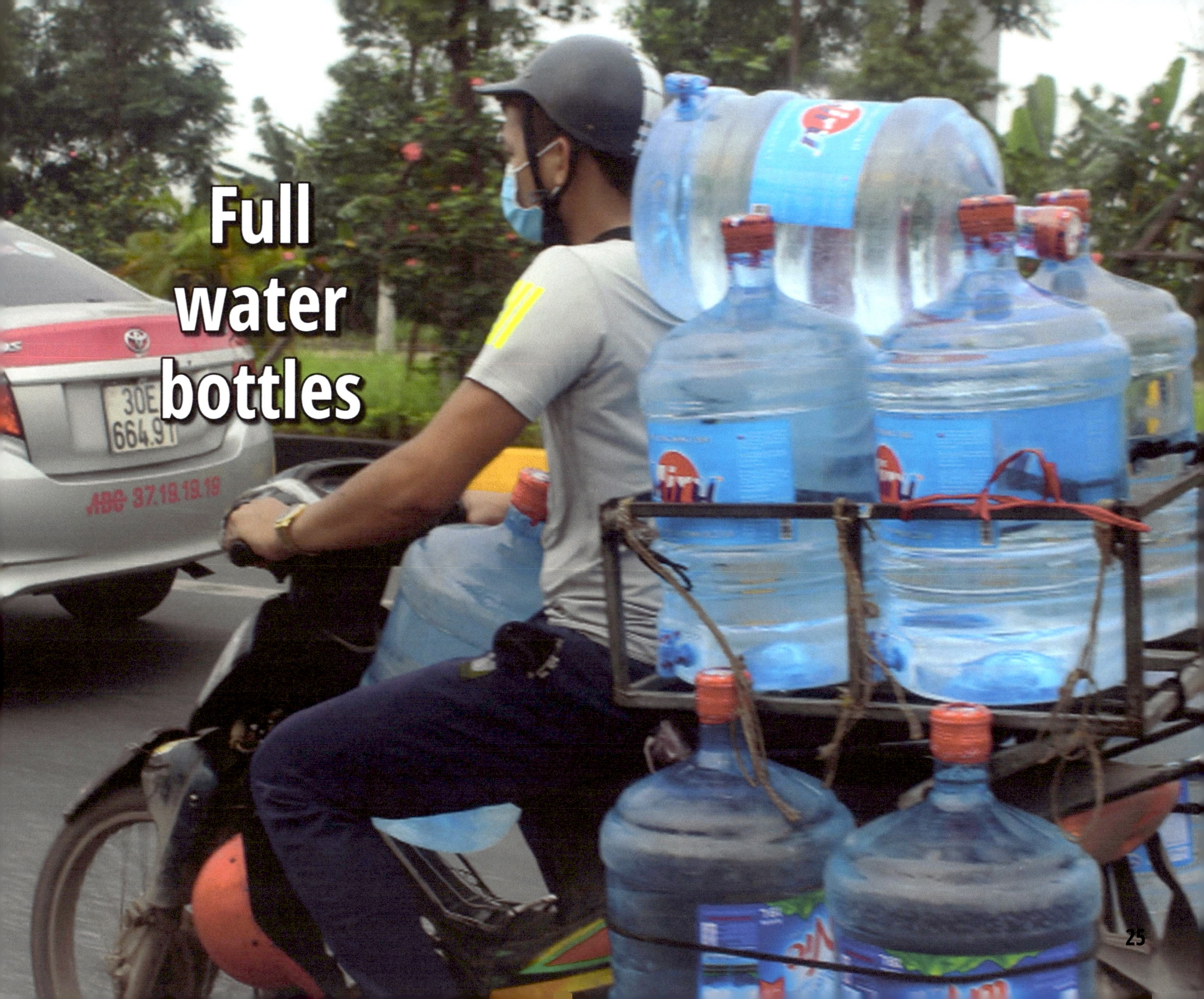

Full
water
bottles

Deluxe trash pick up

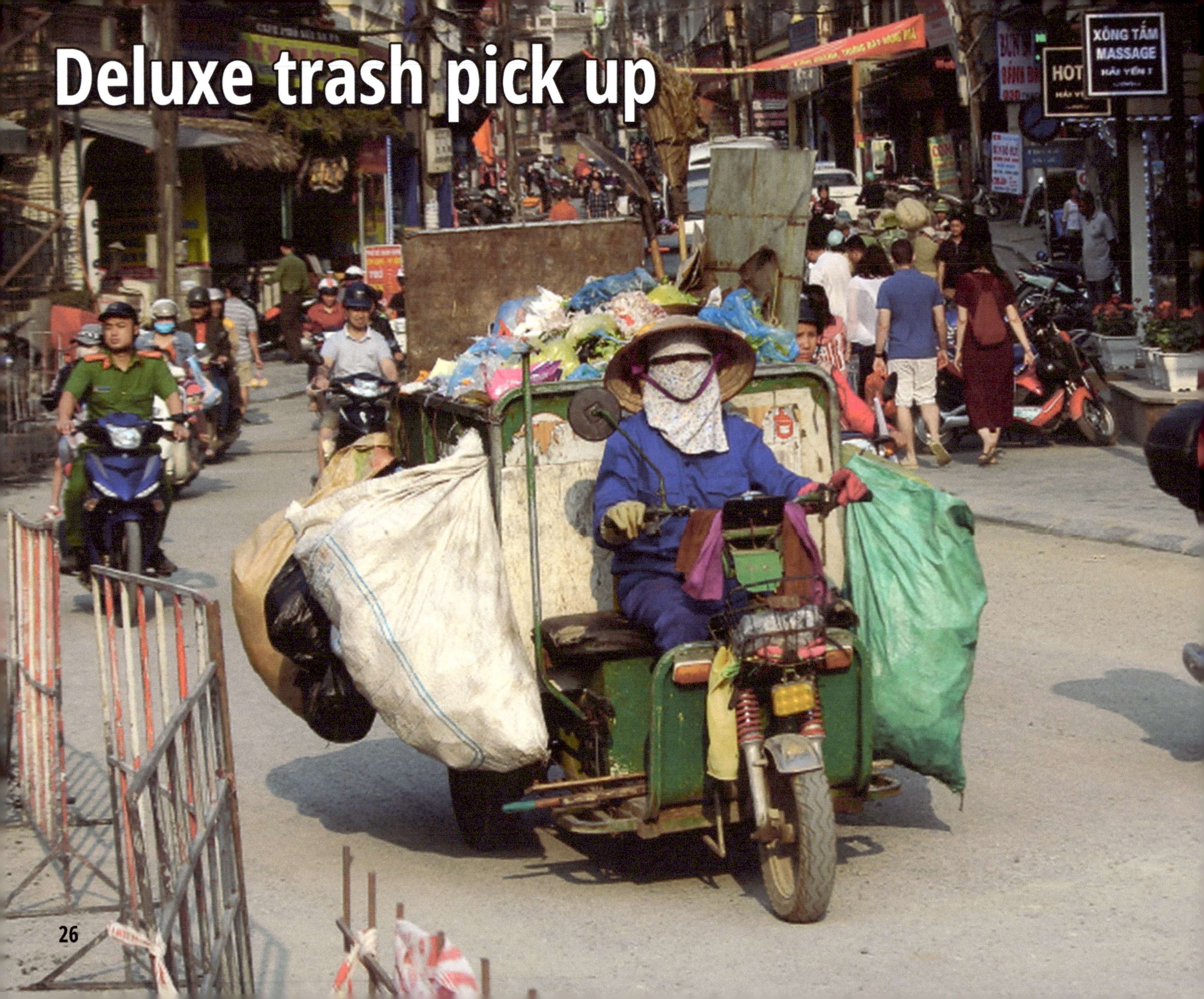

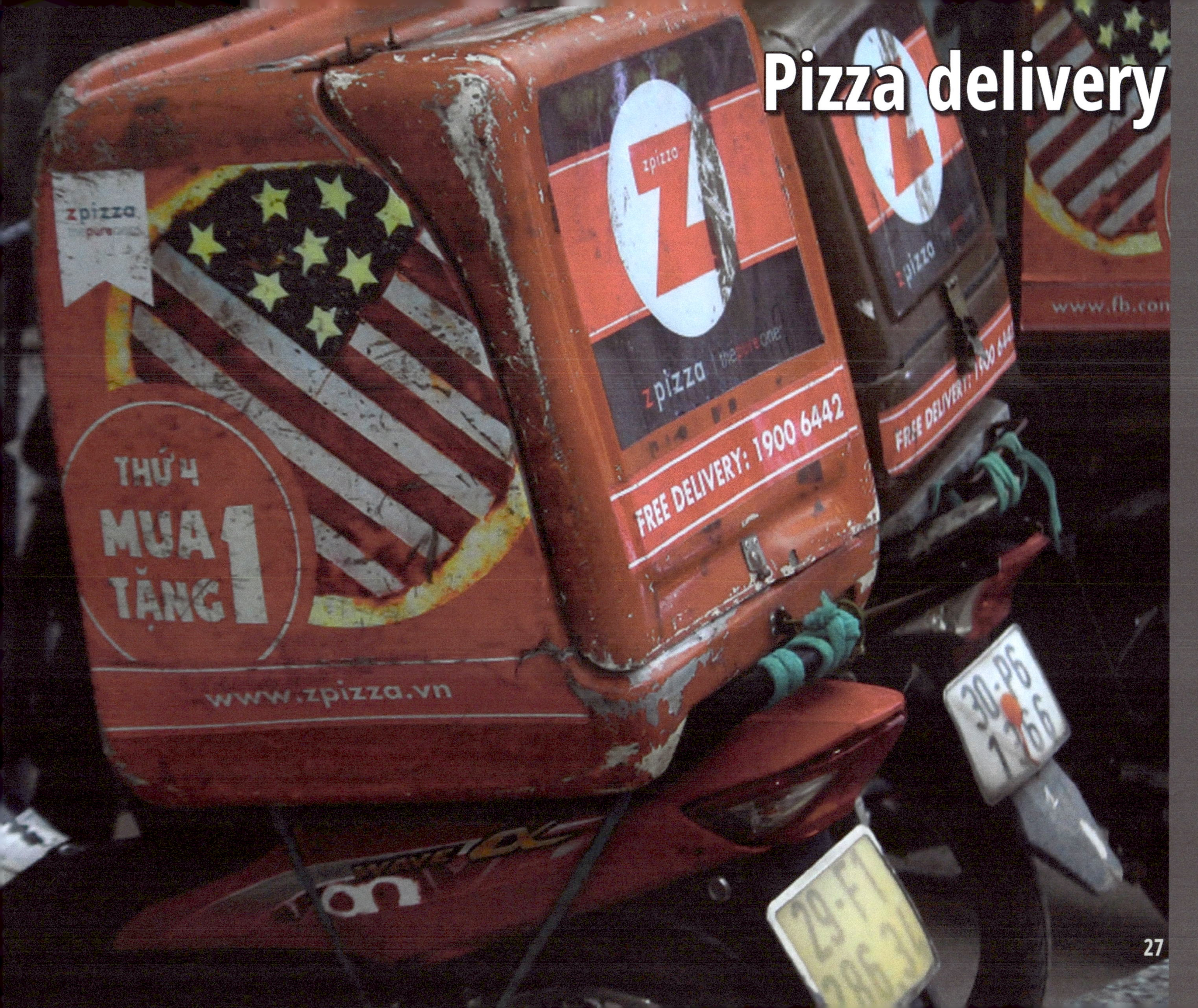

Pizza delivery

zpizza
the pure pizza
THỨ 4
MUA 1
TẶNG 1
www.zpizza.vn
zpizza
zpizza | the pure one
FREE DELIVERY: 1900 6442
FREE DELIVERY: 1900 6442
www.fb.com
30-P6
1 66
29-F1
86 3

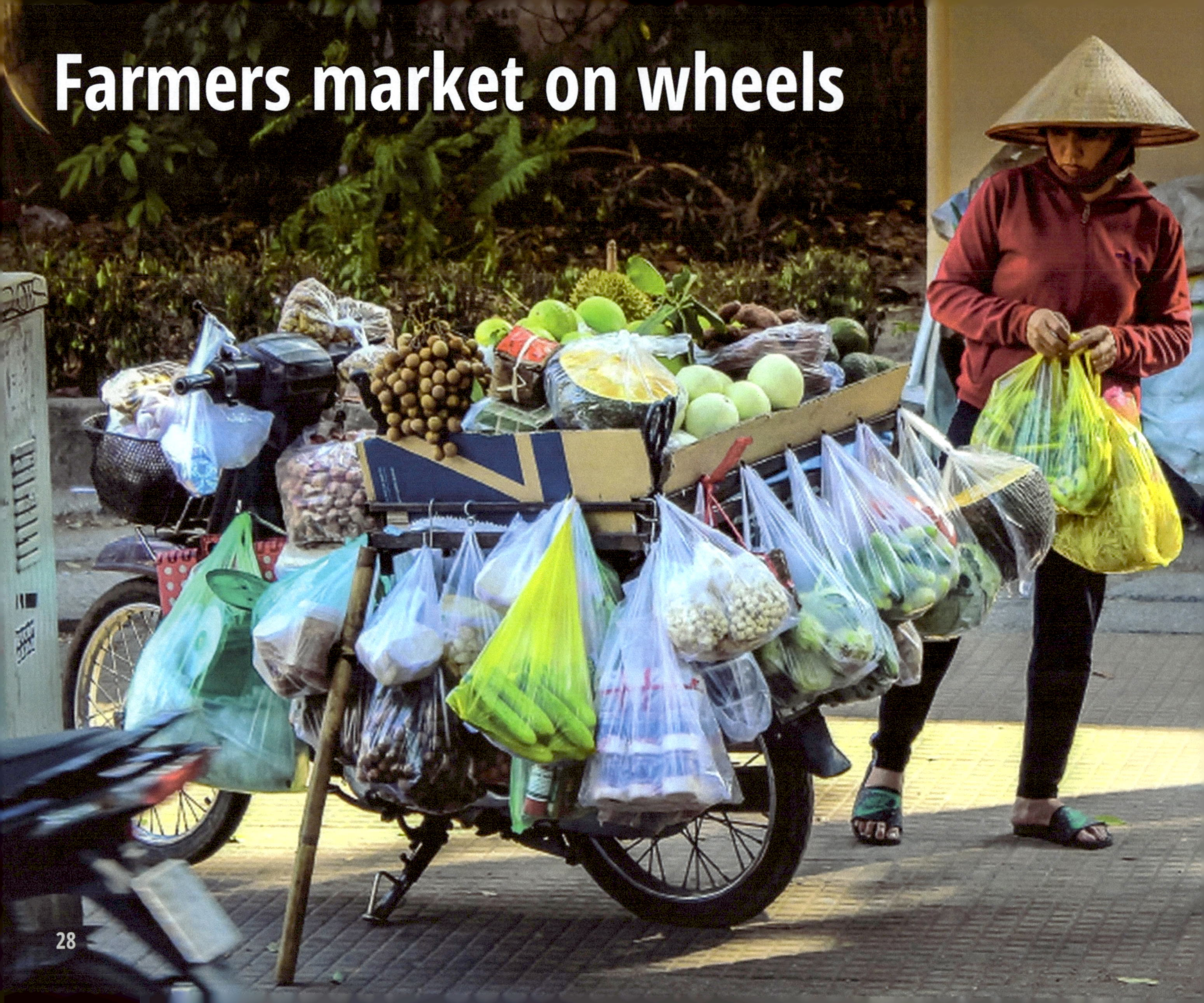

Farmers market on wheels
28

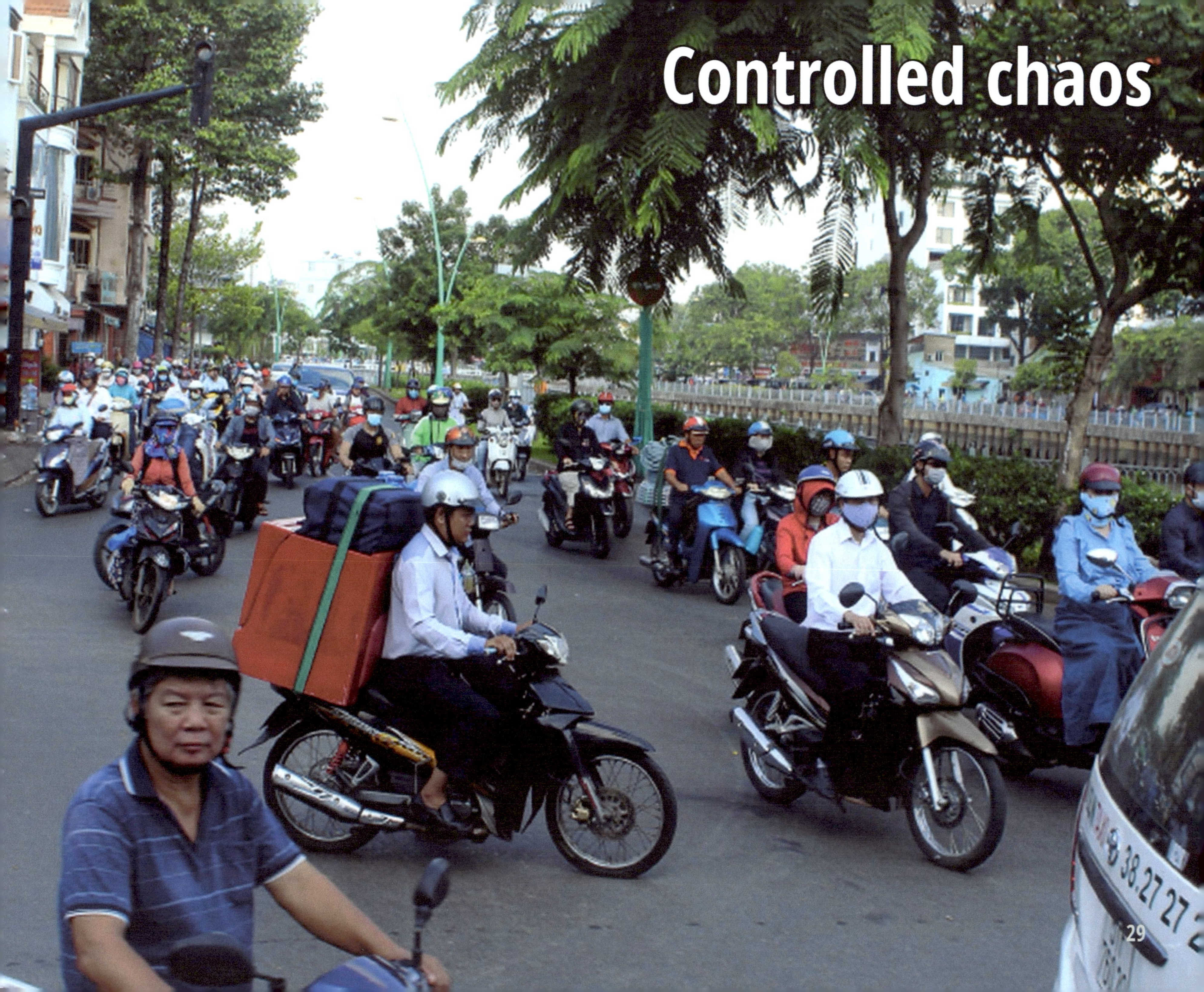

Controlled chaos

Milk men

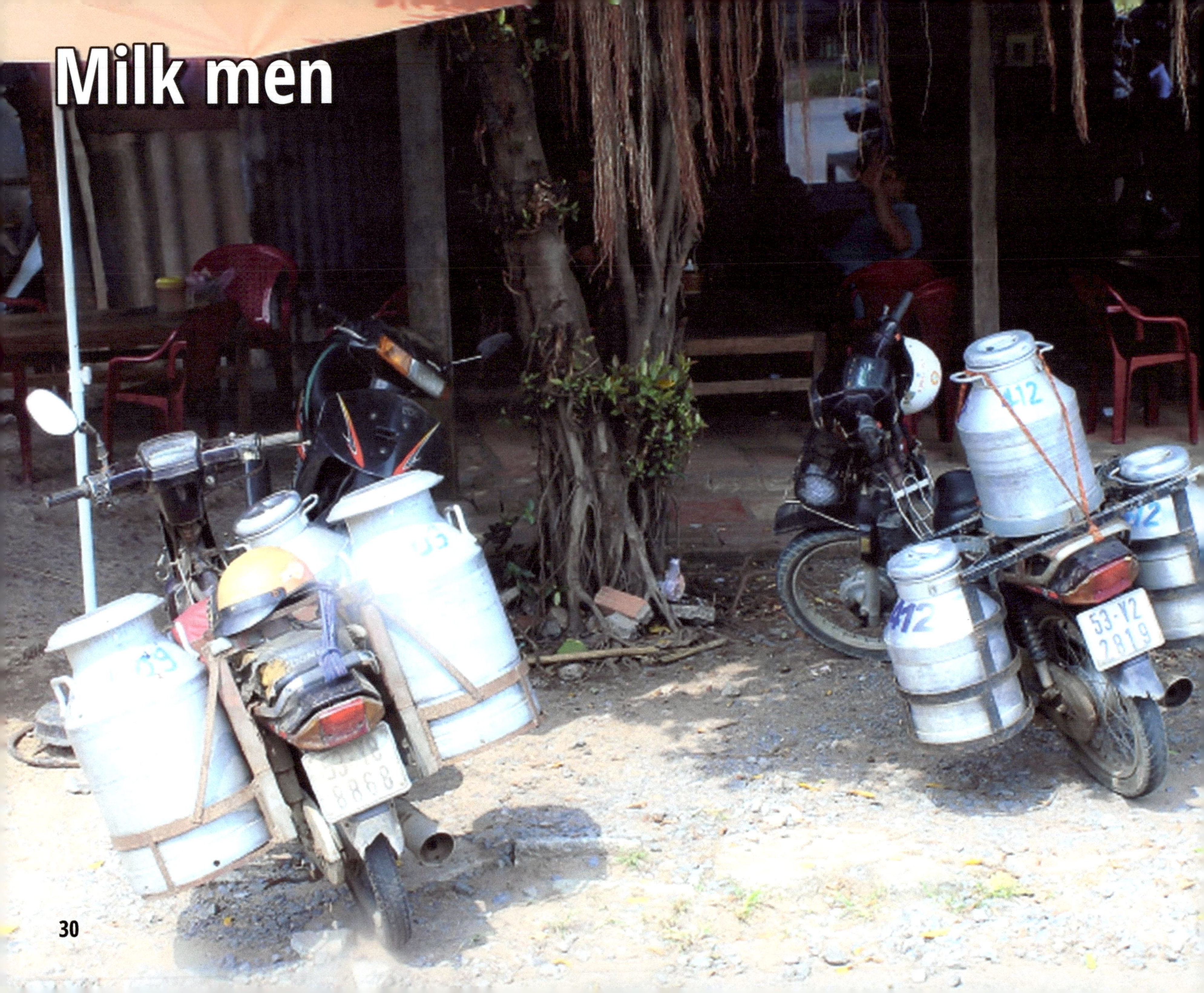

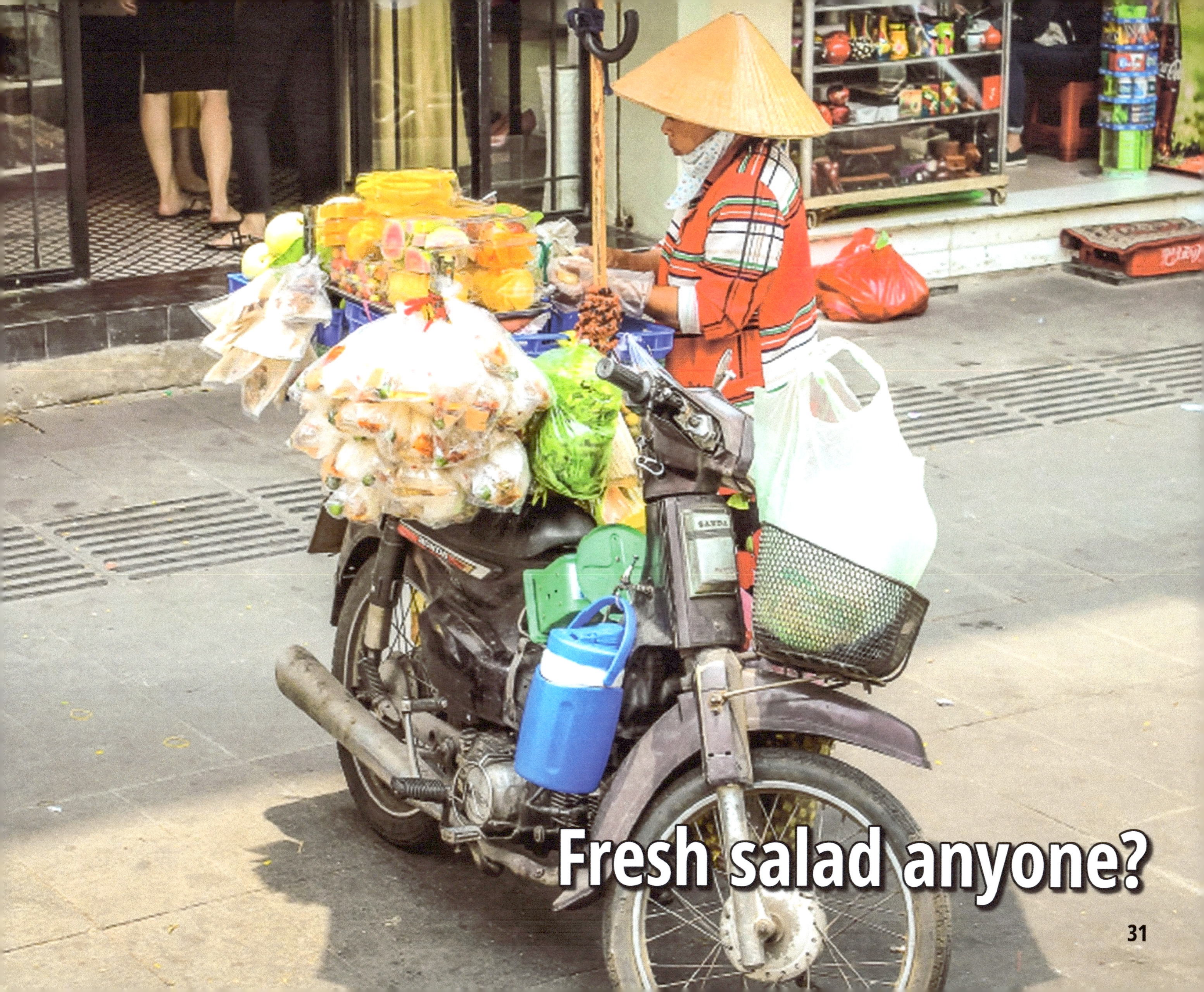
Fresh salad anyone?

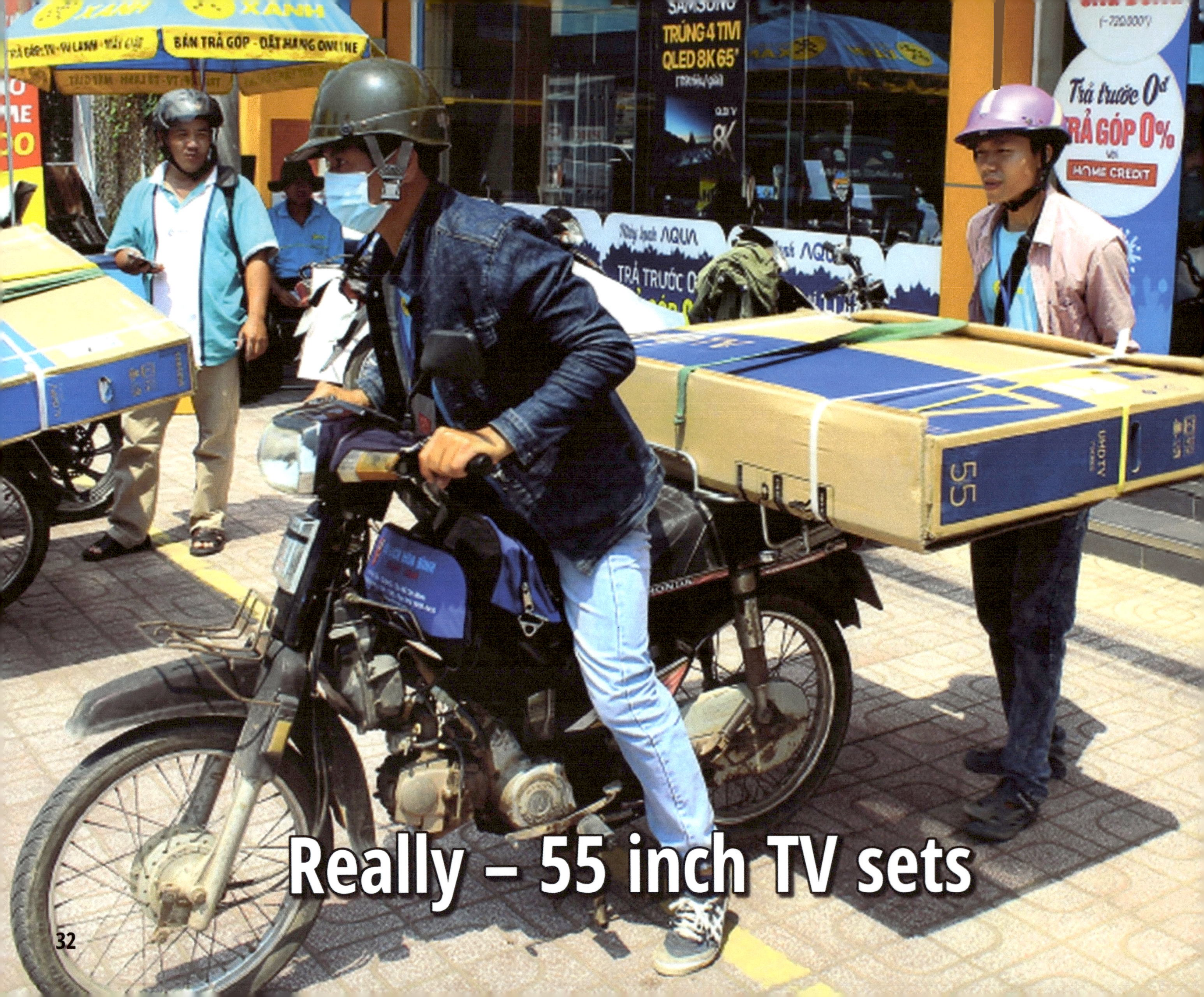
Really – 55 inch TV sets

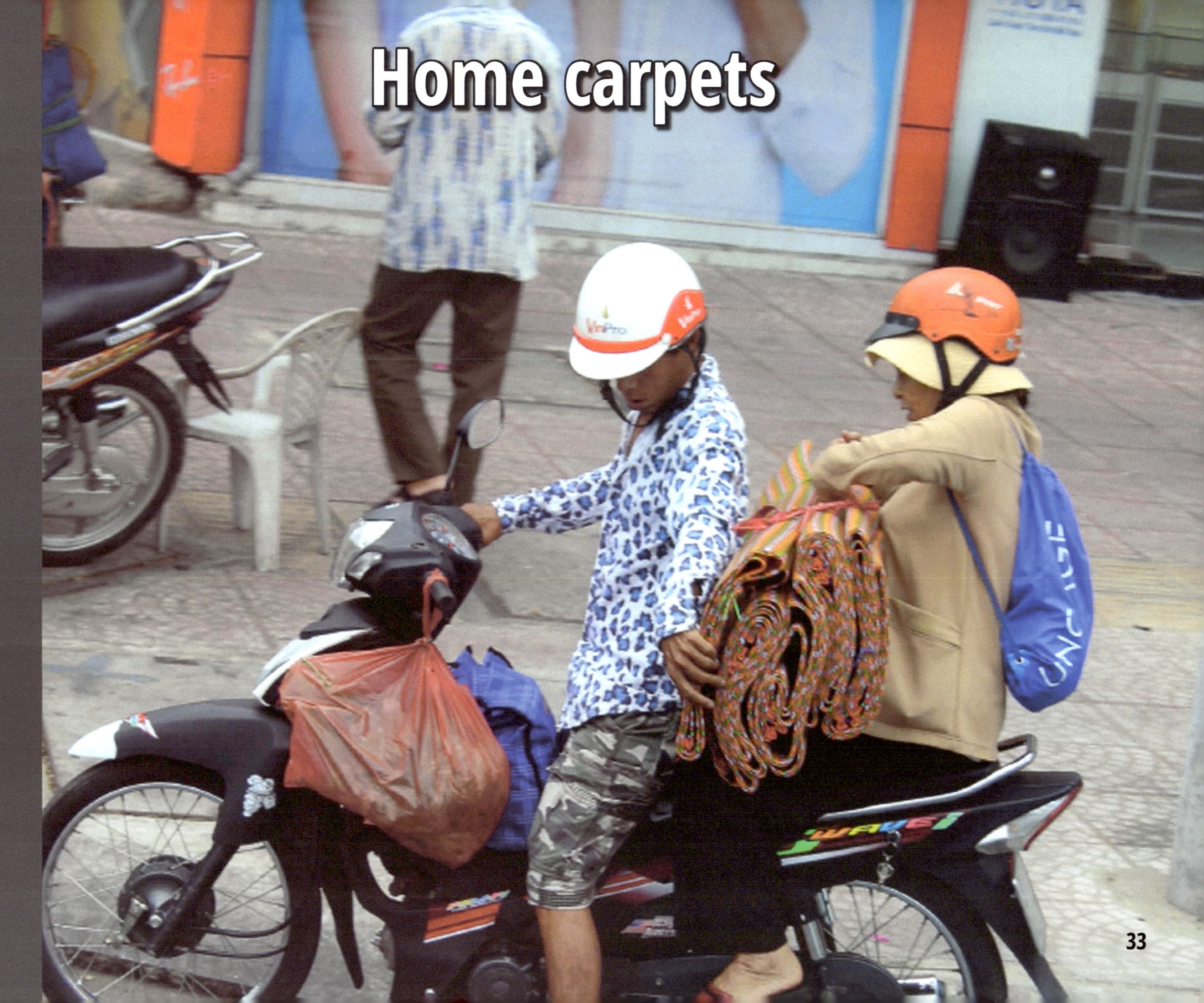
Home carpets

Uber on motorbikes

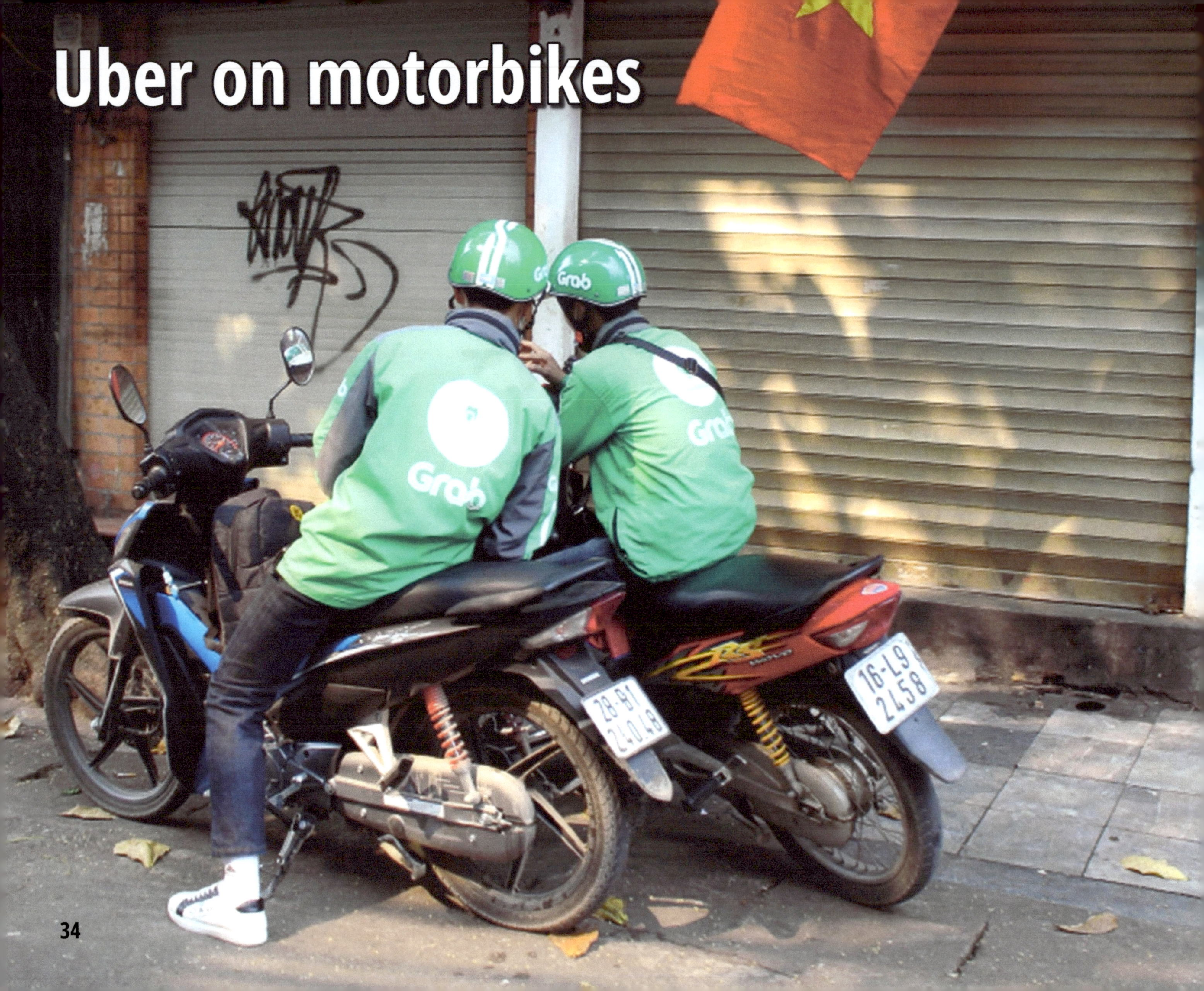

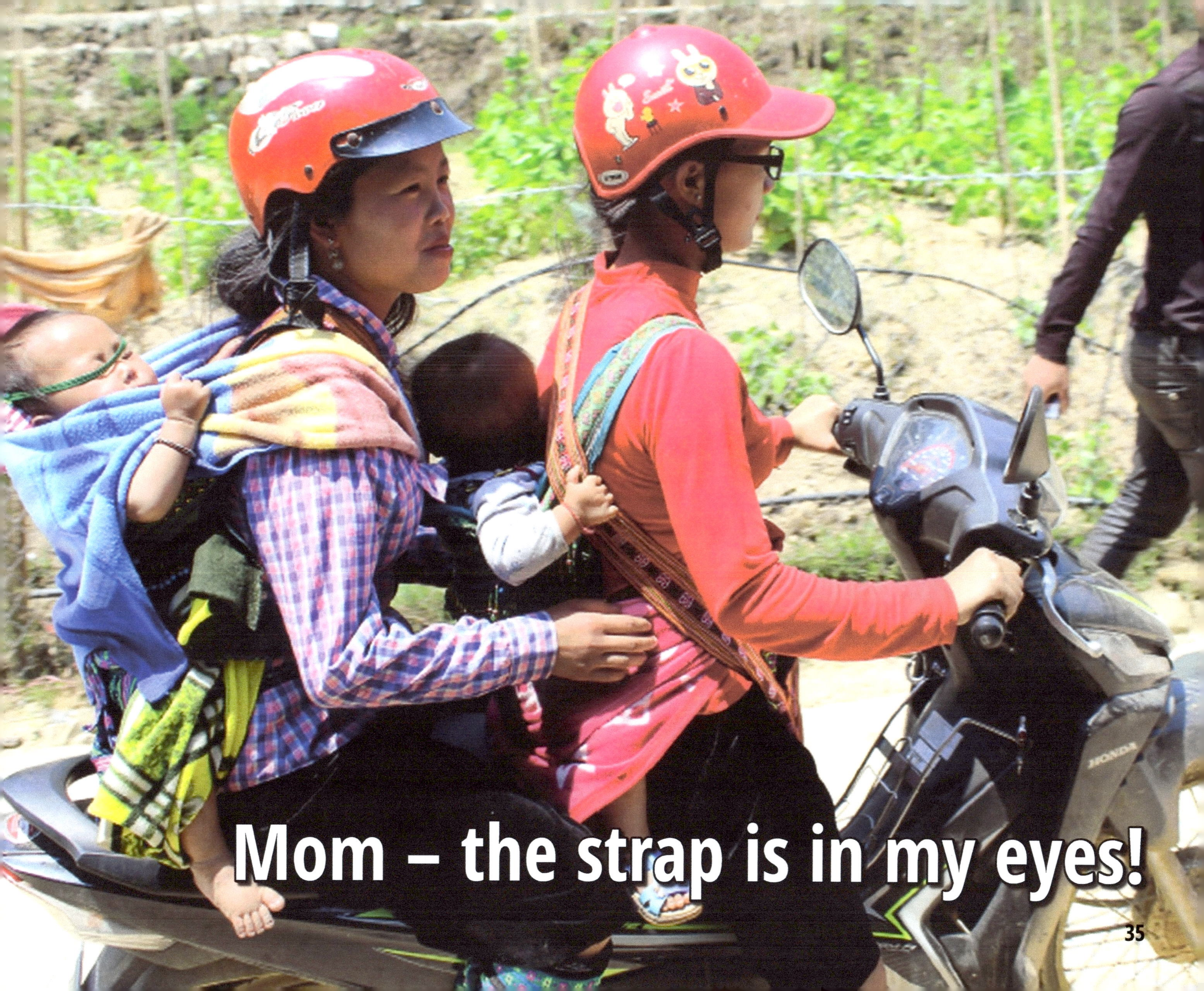

Mom – the strap is in my eyes!

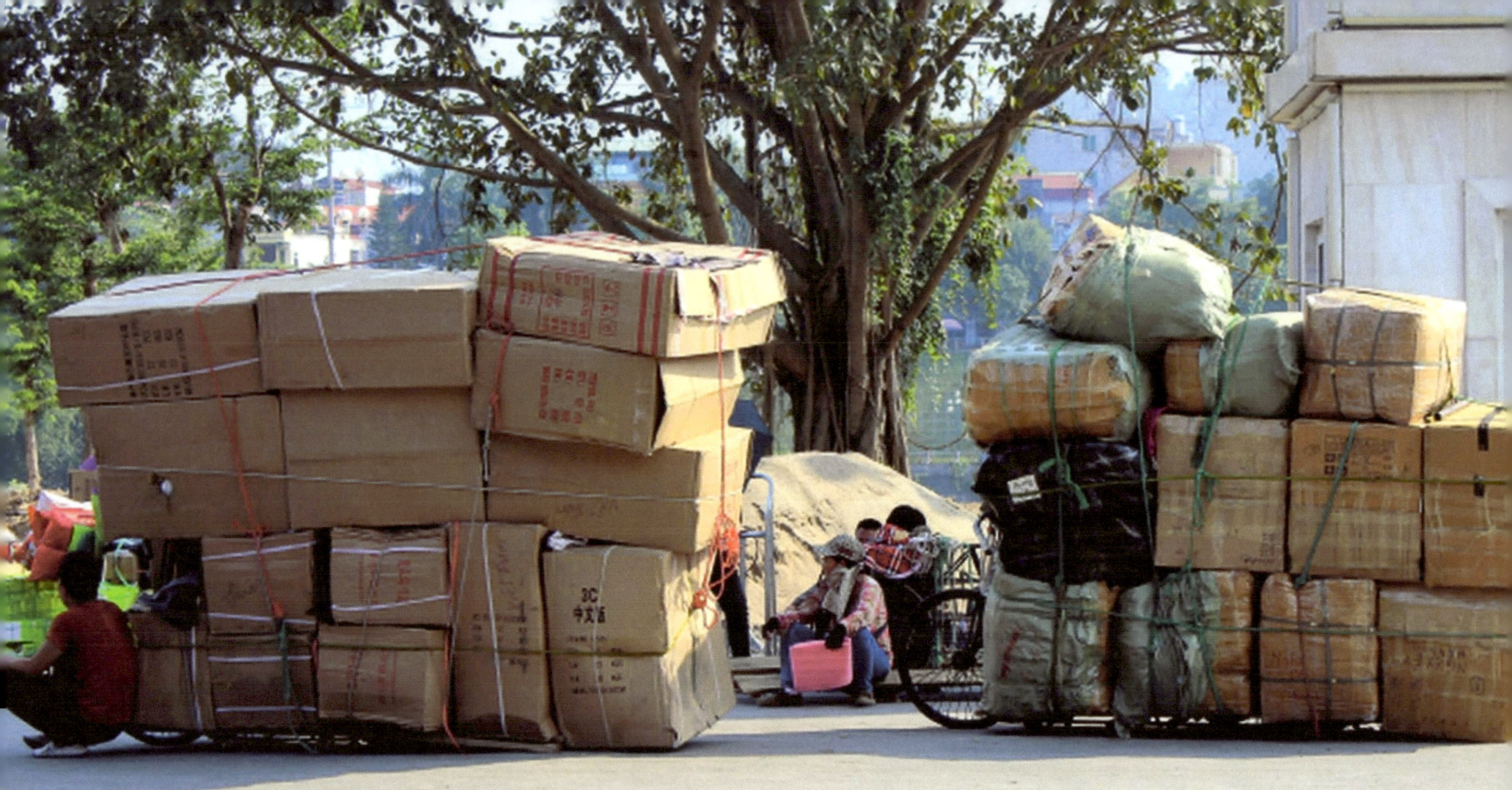

Cargo on motorbikes crossing
into Vietnam from China

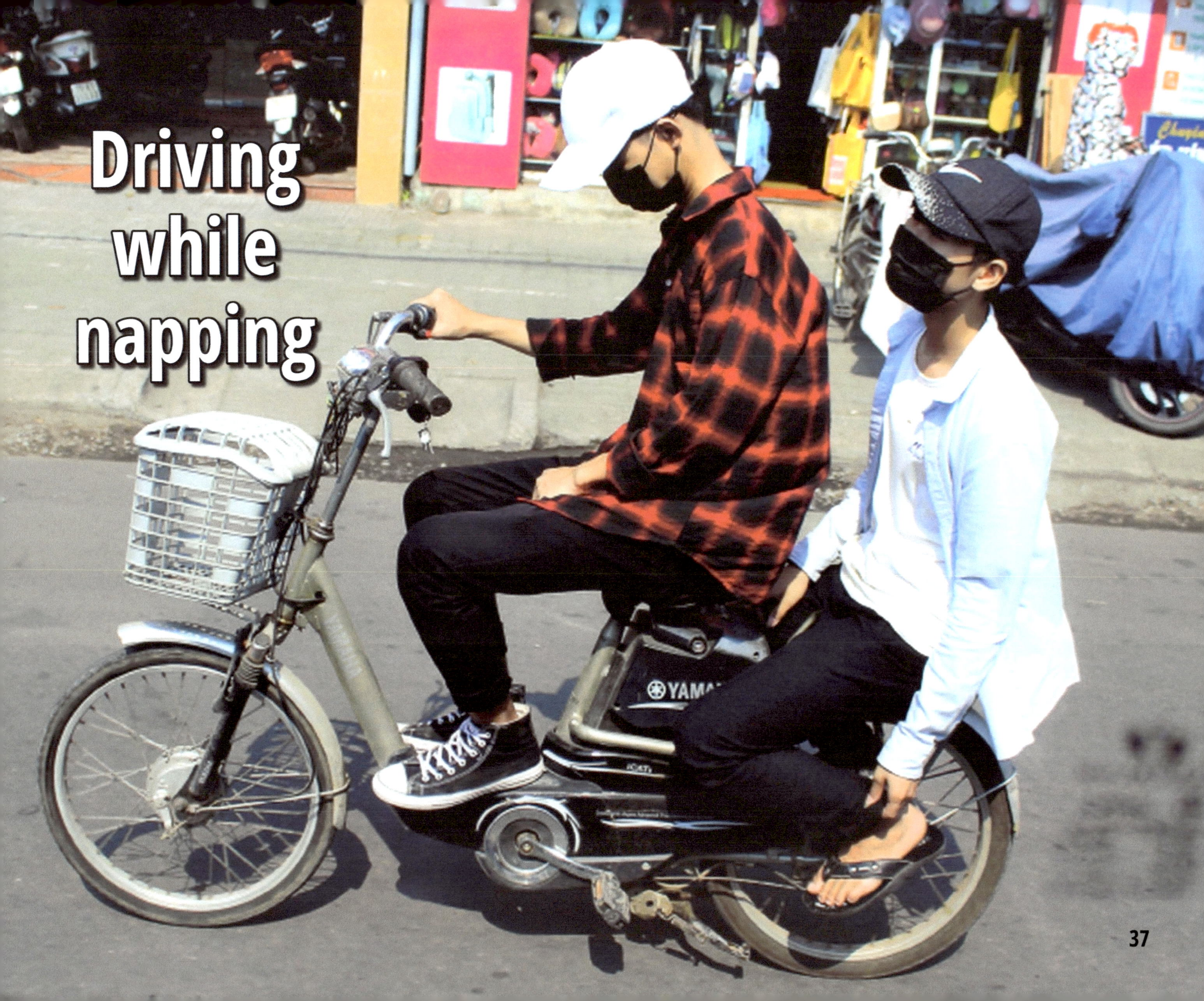

Driving while napping

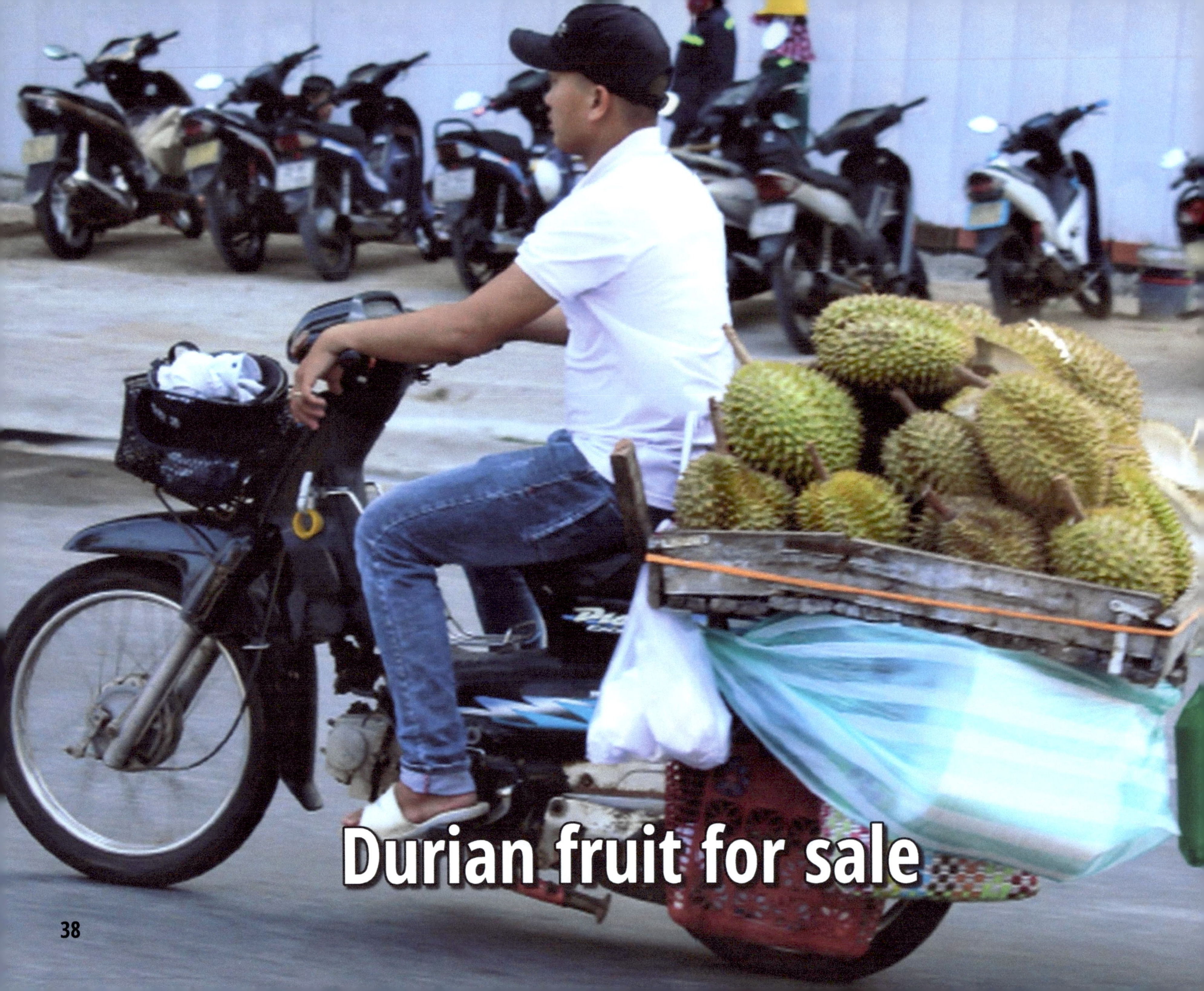

Durian fruit for sale

Distracted driver?

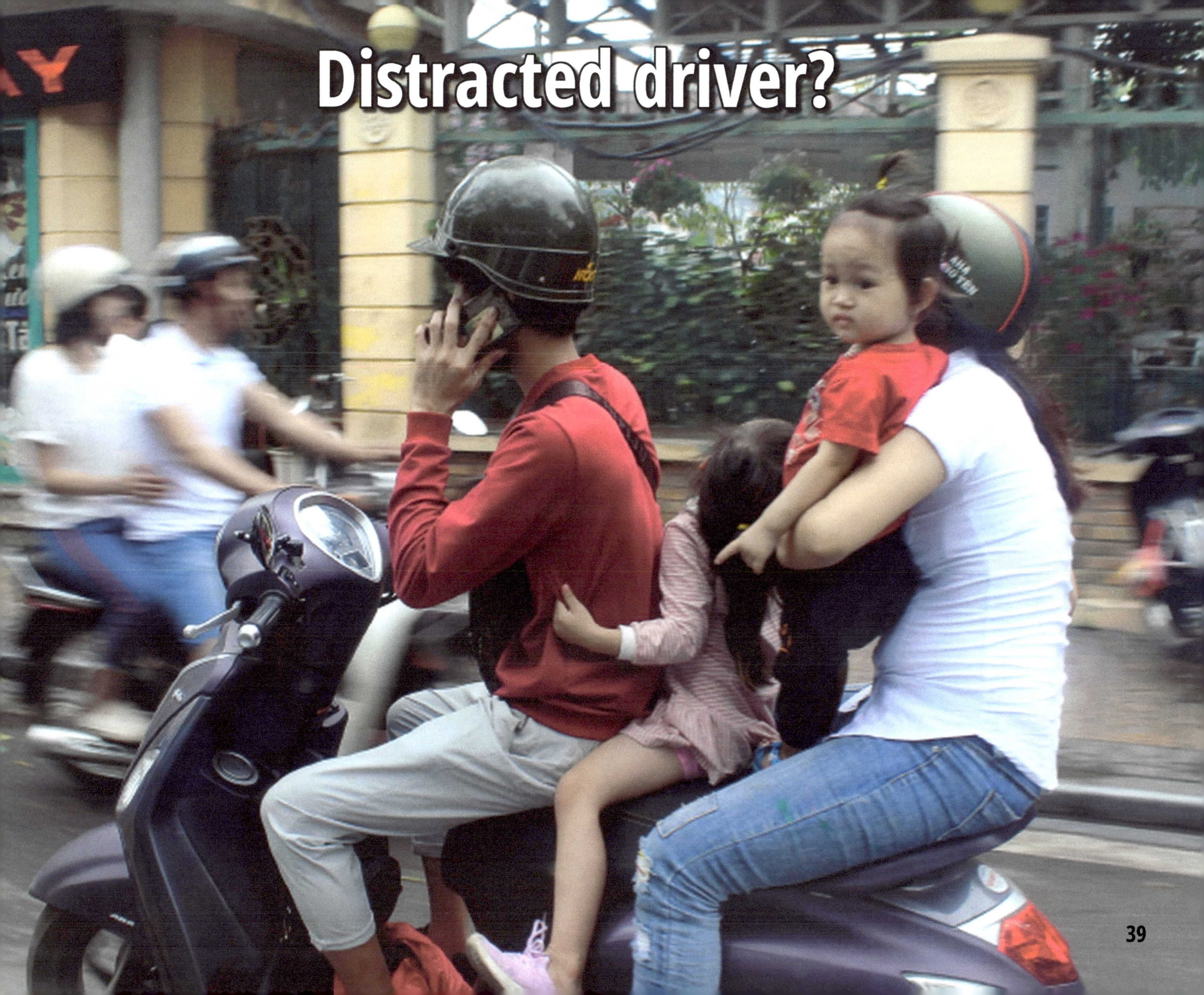

Going home from shopping

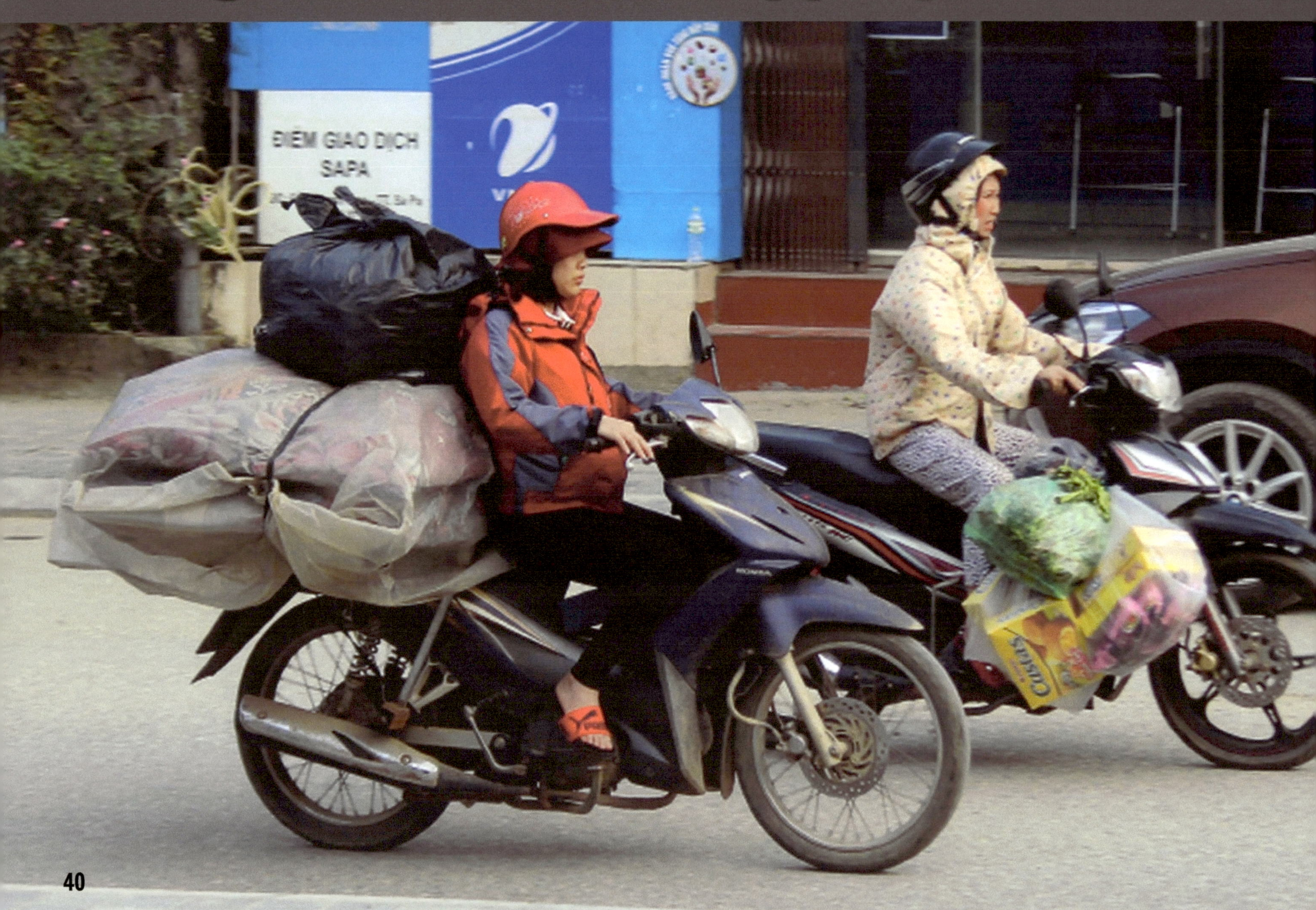

Thomas Auer is a retired family physician who spent 23 years on active duty with the Army Medical Corps. His highly decorated and distinguished career took him to assignments in Wuerzburg, Germany, Ft. Lewis, Wa, Ft. Leonard Wood, MO, the Army War College, Washington, DC, and Ft. Bragg, NC. He retired as a Colonel after serving as the Commander of Womack Army Medical Center, Ft. Bragg. His awards include the Legion of Merit and the Meritorious Service Medal each with two Oak Leaf Clusters and the Order of Military Medical Merit.

His civilian career was just as distinguished and spanned 20 years of leadership positions in private medical groups culminating as the CEO of the Bon Secours Virginia Medical Group in Richmond, VA. He is an avid photographer, traveler, cross country skier, and golfer.

He has been married to Patricia Auer for 49 tremendous years and they have two amazing children, Jef and Alexis, and their spouses, Amaka and Dave, and two fantastic granddaughters, Erica and Adannaya.

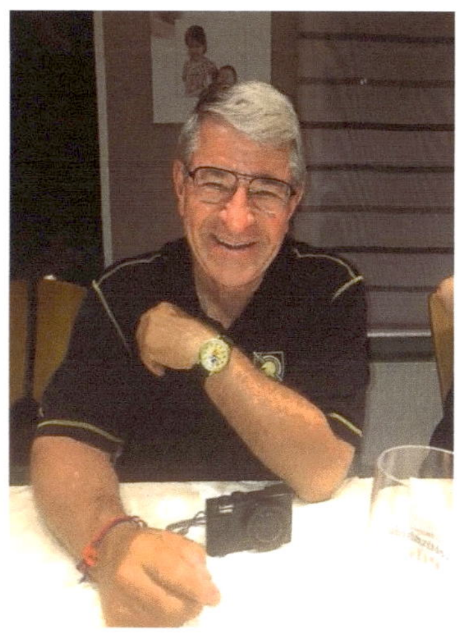